On the Road To Emmaus

Youth devotional journey through Christian faith

Rev. Fr. Abjar Bahkou, Ph.D.

iUniverse, Inc.
Bloomington

On the Road To Emmaus
Youth devotional journey through Christian faith

iUniverse books may be ordered through booksellers or by contacting:

iUniverse
1663 Liberty Drive
Bloomington, IN 47403
www.iuniverse.com
1-800-Authors (1-800-288-4677)

ISBN: 978-1-4620-1670-9 (sc)
ISBN: 978-1-4620-1671-6 (ebook)

Printed in the United States of America

iUniverse rev. date: 05/24/2011

Dedication

To the First Teachers Who Introduced Me to The Christian Faith

To My Mom and Dad, Youssef and Adibah

To Those Who Inspire Me Through My Journey

of Love, Joy, and Hope

To the Syrian Youth in The United States

Contents

FOURTH STATION
THE HOLY CHURCH

Preface

I had never anticipated coming to the United States. I had never expected starting a career in the land of diversity, challenge, richness, and opportunity. I had never imagined to be a youth minister in America!

In 1999, after graduating from the Pontifical Salesian University in Rome, Italy, I was given a mandate to join the Western Archdiocese of the Syrian Orthodox Church in the United States and become a member of its clergy.

Like the first apostles who were trained by our Lord for three years to carry on the message of salvation to the four corners of the earth, I was trained for six years at St. Ephraim Theological Seminary in the Syrian Capital Damascus; and another six years in the Italian Capital of Rome, to be able to carry on the Gospel message to any corner of the world. To my surprise, the Holy Spirit selected California.

With overwhelming emotion and with a sense of fear and eagerness, joy and enthusiasm, I started to serve three communities in Northern and Southern California: St. Thomas Church in San Jose, St. Elias Church in Chico, Sacramento, and St. Paul in San Diego. In addition to the Sunday duties with these three churches and, because of my specialty in youth ministry, I was launched into this jungle.

I started a difficult journey to discover new and healthy paths that would put into practice the theories that I had studied during my twelve years of training in Damascus and Rome. Although I was optimistic, I had to face the difficulties, delusions and illusions of pastoral duties in general and I had to face in particular, the challenges of youth ministry in America.

I wanted, much like the apostle Peter, to get off the boat and walk on the water, but would doubt when I would see the wind of temptations and challenges and I would drown! As peter did, I would vow to follow Jesus and to carry on His message, yet with the first confrontation I would deny Him three times! However, I would always sense Jesus' hands extend to me, bruising and binding me up, wounding and making me whole (Job 5: 18). His left hand scolding me, "You of little faith, why do you doubt?" and His right hand encouraging me, "Take courage! Don't be afraid."

Through this pastoral and personal journey, I realized the needs of our community to form professional committees and organizations that would be able to produce new methods, curricula, and plans for our youth. I saw an urgent need in our community for a book that could help our youth understand the basics of our Christian faith and learn how to apply these basics to daily life.

While I prepared lectures, sermons, and Bible studies, the idea of writing a book came to mind. My passion for a healthy youth ministry and my vision to better integrate our youth into the life of the Church inspired me even further.

I started to write small notes on the Christian faith and discuss it in our youth meetings and see the youth feedbacks to the notes and the questions that I asked, I did this for almost two years, the outcome was this book. This introductory curriculum is the product of intense daily work with the youth of our Orthodox parishes in Los Angeles, Orange County, San Bernardino, and Chico.

In the beginning of 2003, I finished writing this book and I thought it was ready to be published. Well, I was mistaken, because I repeated the same fault of getting quickly out off the boat and running on the water, doubting and, consequently, drowning. I needed to stay in the "upper room" for a time of devotions, reflections and longing for the Holy Spirit. Like Moses, I needed to get out of Egypt and wander in the wilderness in order to be able to clear my vision, shape up my calling and meet the Burning Bush.

From the year 2003 till the beginning of 2005 I left the ministry and I took another job. I thought I was not called to be a minister anymore! I left the Church full of anger, resentment, and rejection, and I started to wonder and seek another calling. In 2004 I left California and moved to Fort Worth, Texas to look for a new adventure, new land,

and to seek peace in my life. In August 2004 I started a new academic endeavor at Brite Divinity School at Texas Christian University where I was enrolled in the Master in Theological Studies program, after finishing two semesters at the above mentioned school, I moved to Southwest Baptist Theological Seminary in Fort Worth where I graduated with the Master in Mission and Evangelism. Then worked as a research assistant, and later, as instructor at the above mentioned Seminary. for the last two years I am a full time lecturer of Arabic Language and culture at Baylor University, Waco Texas.

Through this journey, the Lord, in His compassion and mercy, showed me that I am called to ministry; I am chosen to be His priest and servant, and I have a mandate to carry on His message of salvation to the four corners of the earth.

Since 2005 the Lord has opened new spiritual and theological horizons in front of me. The Holy Spirit allowed me to preach in many different places here in America and in other countries such as Sweden, Switzerland, Canada, and Syria.

After two years of reflection, travels, and devotions, the Lord stretched out His hand again and encouraged me to share this journey. Thus, this curricula is part of my personal journey. I poured my heart and spirit into it. It is not a pure theological essay, but a blend of experience and theology. The fathers of the Church throughout history underlined two important conditions in studying the Bible and writing theology: the first is to *read the Bible communally within Christ's body, the Church.* The exegesis is an ecclesial task that takes place within the Church and for the Church. The second is to *read the Bible within the context of practice of prayer, worship and spiritual formation.* The fathers insisted on the connection between spiritual well being, life in the Church and commentary on the Church book. I have faithfully endeavored to follow the instructions of the fathers.

My hope is that the reader of this book, or the group that will share this journey, will realize that this voyage is the culmination of almost 10 years of daily reflection and analysis of the problems that our teenagers face in their daily lives. It is the reply to many prayers and personal devotions. Its ultimate purpose is to help our youth build a personal and intimate relationship with our Lord Jesus Christ.

Writing a book is difficult; no one can deny that. However, writing a book that instructs our youth about their religion and faith is even more difficult. I offer my continuous thanksgiving to the Lord Almighty, who applied the journey of Emmaus to my life and allowed me to share it with our youth in North America.

Many thank to my mother-in-love Anna peters and my wife Phylan Bahkou, my student Caterina Riley for their suggestions and help in the editing process.

Quotations from Scriptures are from the New International Version.

My endless prayer is that this book will be a helpful guide for our youth in the United States to understand and practice their Christian faith, and to be able to inspire others.

Rev. Fr. Abjar Bahkou, Ph.D.
Hurst, Texas 2011

Leader's Notes

Then we will no longer be infants, tossed back and fourth by the waves, and blown here and there by every wind of teaching and by cunning and craftiness of men in their deceitful scheming. Instead... we will in all things grow up into Him Who is the head that is Christ (Ephesians 4: 14 – 26, NIV).

We proclaim Him, admonishing and teaching everyone with all wisdom, so that we may present everyone perfect in Christ. To this end I labor struggling with all His energy which so powerfully works in me (Colossians 1: 24, NIV).

1. General Message

This is not a book to hand out to the youth when they need help in their struggle. It is a walk, or a journey, that a student will not be able to walk alone. The ideas presented in this introductory curriculum are not meant to simply feed students some information about Christian life, but rather they are seeds that need to be nurtured. Such a nurturing process is done through Christian mentors and a community of believers that can facilitate and encourage this developing process.

What is the general message of this book? This devotional youth program intends:

- To shape a mature personality within the adolescent by which faith becomes part of his daily life, as St. Paul described it in his letter to the Ephesians: "We will in all things grow up into Him Who is the head, that is Christ" (Ephesians 4: 15).
- To help youth understand the basics of the Christian Faith and how to apply it to their daily lives.

The curriculum suggests some figures and experiences from the Bible that uphold the presence of God in the history of humanity. These Biblical patterns intend to help youth:

- Discover God's "promises" and "plan" as an invitation of friendship to each one of them.
- Discern through the persons and experiences of the Holy Scriptures the various forms by which God calls us to participate with Him in His divine plan.

- Distinguish that all the experiences and prophecies of the Old Testament focus on one major event, which is the coming of our Lord Jesus Christ. And also to realize that Jesus Christ is the One who guides us to make the right choices in life.
- Renew and develop the gifts of the Holy Spirit.
- Answer with confidence the call of God as Abraham, Isaac, Joseph, and Moses did. Develop courageous and faithful tendencies toward Christian life.

2. Pastoral-Educational goals

Chap Clark, the associate professor of Youth and Family Ministry at Fuller Theological Seminary in Pasadena, California, in his article *youth Ministry in an age of delayed adulthood,* explains the term of adolescence which was a new term created in 1800, "Adolescence stems from Latin *adolscer* meaning "to grow up." The idea of a time when a person is no longer child but not yet an adult." Clark divide the adolescence in three stages, 1) Early adolescence (Junior High, roughly 10–14 years Old), 2) middle adolescence (Senior High, 14-17/19 years old), 3) Late adolescence (college and young adult 17/19 to mid–to-late 20s).

Stage 1: Early adolescence

1. **The important of family.** Because an early adolescent is more a child than an adult, the family still plays the major role of identification and security.
2. **Safety, priority #1.** We don't have to think of how much fun the program is, but we have to realize how save they feel, how we treat them from up front.

3. **Fitting in.** To most early adolescents, the only thing that really matters is how they perceive themselves fitting in.

Stage 2: Middle adolescence

1. **The importance of friendships.** Middle adolescents who lives in a culture where adult systems have abandoned them to discover rules, norms, values, and lifestyle choice on their own, friends play a far more significant role in their lives than in a previous decades.
2. **Family still matters, but in a different way.** They long to find themselves and make their own decisions while still being connected to their families. We must work to help families during these times of struggle.
3. **Huge swing in commitment levels are normal.** This is a time to learn from the swing in emotion, in loyalties, and in commitments. We must allow middle adolescent to be middle adolescent, and not try to force them into superficial of feigned level of premature commitment and responsibility.
4. **The need for immediate perceived relevance in all aspect of the program.** Because they are middle abstract teaching and concepts must be grounded in perceived reality and everyday experience.
5. **Every kid need and older friend/mentor.** Because many kids today feel abandoned by adult systems and relationships, they need older friends.

Stage 3: the late adolescence

1. **They are still adolescents.** The vast majority of college students and working, young

adults are still adolescents. This means they need foundational teaching, directive adult leadership, and careful theological reflection and mentoring.

2. **They need a gentle shove into adulthood.** They have to acknowledge who they are before the Lord, seeking their identity in relation to him and taking full responsibilities for how they respond to God and His Word.

3. The Method

When God the Father wanted to touch our lives, He sent Jesus the Son, who become a human being like us and shared our pain. We call this *Incarnation.*

The incarnation stands as a foundational principle for effective Christian Education of teens. *As God sought to reach us by entering our world and journeying with us, so we must enter the world of young people and journey with them.* St. Paul understood this approach well. He wrote that when he wanted to reach the Jews, he became like the Jews, and when he wanted to reach the Gentiles, he became like the Gentiles (1 Corinthians 9: 19 – 23).

To be effective in youth discipleship, we have to earn the right to be heard by building relationships with young people, we are seen as credible and caring people, worthy of their trust.

Relational or Incarnational Christian Education needs three aspects:

1. Be personally present to youth. We need to go where young people spend their time. As leaders we need to ask, "where are the teens?". Our response to this question will reveal the best location for a Christian Education. Such places might includes the local high school, sporting events, plays, concerts, the mall, the park, fast food restaurants, gyms, and arcades.

Youth need to see us on their ground. The word that Jesus used for the great commission was "Go"; in other words, *we must move out of our comfort zone and initiate outreach*. We often replace "Go" with "come", and simply set up in the church doing our best to "save the choir." The problem with this approach is that we are only reaching a small percentage of teens, usually those teens who need to be there.

2. Enter the world of the adolescent. The real challenge before us is learning how to enter the complex and confused world of today's youth, and make relational connections at a deep and emotional level that no cultural influence will able to destroy.

We must connect with our kids relationally and emotionally if we are going to salvage this generation. Yet, many adults today are focusing in another area. They are trying to protect their children from the Godless culture and teach them the truth by providing tougher rules and firmer guidance. But rules, regulations, and instructions alone will not produce the desired result.

We must instruct and counsel our kids within the context of a relational connection, an emotional attachment, and a loving bond in our daily interaction with them. Only then will the rules and instructions we provide be meaningful and fruitful in their lives.

The world of a teenager is a very different one from the adult world. Our aim is not to try and make young people officially authorized adults. We do not want to force them to enter into the world of the adult, but rather to venture forth into their domain and journey with them.

A teen's world and issues can seem trivial, foolish, or incomprehensible to an adult mind, but youth ministry is a missionary calling. Adults are called forth from their own familiar culture and civilized ways of thinking into the uncharted jungle of the modern youth mindset and culture.

3. Journey with young people. We must be willing to partner with teens on their journey. In order to be truly effective, we can not simply meet with them an hour a week, attempting to religiously saturate their minds with the glorious truths of the church. Effective youth ministry and Christian education involves long-term relationships. We need to channel more of our efforts toward becoming people-centered as opposed to program-centered.

All too often, our relationships with the teens begin and end with the program. If we operate only on a program-centered model, we then reach youth with only the content of the meeting. With a people-centered model we reach them with the content of our love brought to life by our words, examples and actions. A people-centered for youth ministry most certainly offers programs. The difference is that the ministry goes beyond the reaches of organized church programming and into the realm of real life our love brought to life by our words. This, in turn, helps teens understand that faith is a way of living that is integrated into all of life.

There are at least six biblically based relational connecting points[1] we can make with our young people that will shape and mold them mentally, emotionally, and spiritually.

1. Affirmation. One of the most often-used phrases by young people is: "they don't understand me." When young people don't feel that you identify with them, they are less likely to stay connected to you emotionally. And one of the most effective ways to identify with them, even when you don't fully understand them, is to *affirm their feeling.*

To affirm means "to validate or confirm." When we affirm the feelings of our young people, we give them a sense of authenticity. Affirming their feeling tells them that they are real individuals with valid feelings. When we identify with their feelings of excitement or disappointment, we let them know they are understood for who they really are

2. Acceptance. When we accept young people for who they are, we give them a sense of security. Acceptance deals more with *embracing people for who they are rather than for what they do.* When your young people feel accepted by you, they are more likely to be vulnerable and transparent, opening up greater trust with you. Your acceptance helps

1 Cf. Josh McDowell, *The Disconnected Generation,* Word Publishing, Nashville 2000, 47-121.

your kids believe that no matter what happens, you will still love them. An accepting relationship creates a loving bond and intimate relational connection between you and your student.

3 Appreciation. When we express appreciation to young people, we give them a sense of significance. While accepting is the foundation for a secure relationship, appreciation can be considered a cornerstone. Our acceptance of young people tells them that their being matters. Expressing our appreciation to them says that their doing matters too. Our appreciation conveys to young people that they are valued and that their accomplishments do make a difference to someone. It causes them to sense, "Hey, I'm worth something to someone! These adults like having me around and they are proud of me."

4. Affection. When we show affection to young people, we give them a sense of lovability. Expressing affection to our kids through loving words and appreciate touch communicates that they are worth loving. Every expression of care and closeness provides emotional reinforcement, helping kids realize that they are loved.

5. Availability. When we make ourselves available to young people, we give them a sense of importance. And when we are not available, we are saying, in essence: "Oh yes, I love you, but other things still come ahead of you. You are not really that important." Expressing affirmation, acceptance, appreciation, and affection to our kids is critical, but we can only do that if we make ourselves available to them. Being there when your young people need you will not only tell them they are important to you, it will keep you relationally connected to them.

6. *Accountability.* To connect relationally, we need to show our young people affirmation, acceptance, appreciation, affection, and availability. Yet, if we do not balance these relational connection points with loving limits and boundaries, young people will not learn responsibility. When we provide the parameters within which a young person can operate safely and securely. Young people need the loving authority of parents and caring adults so they can learn to make responsible and right choices. Without parameters, there is only confusion and chaos.

God has provided us with these relational connecting points. In scripture we learn that God has demonstrated these connections in the life and ministry of His Son. Christ in fact does Affirm us (Heb. 2: 17 – 18), accept us (Rom. 15: 7), show us appreciation (Matt. 3: 17), lavish us with affection (1John 4: 7), make himself available to us (Ps. 145: 18), and hold us lovingly accountable (Rom. 14: 12). As we follow His example in relationship with our youth and Children, we can establish and maintain the vital relational connections God intended.

The purpose of this curriculum is to implement the relational method. This method, as we have seen, is based on faith and the Word of God, nurtured by a worshipping community of believers.

Being an adolescent is one phase or stage in human life in which a person faces, on a daily basis, changes and developments. Therefore, the question that we as leaders must ask is twofold: first, how can we help them build a positive outlook towards life? And second, how can we facilitate the understanding of faith as an experience of communion with the Lord?

Through our guidance, our students will discover God's call for them, and learn about the history of salvation that started with the story of "the Fall." They will also learn about the salvation that has been realized through the coming of our Lord Jesus Christ, and fulfilled through His death and resurrection. The participants will realize that this story of salvation is still continuing in their lives as well.

The students will learn to appreciate their body and personality as God's gift. They will also explore God's love for them and the way of real freedom, despite all forms of suffering and sin in the world. God's call that was addressed to Abraham, Isaac, and Jacob is the same call that is addressed to today's Christians. It is a call that leads to liberation from sin and evil. Such a call requires that we live out the holy gifts of the new covenant that we received through Jesus

Christ. He is the fulfillment of all the prophecies that God proclaimed to the people of the Old Testament.

Just as Jesus Christ walked with the disciples of Emmaus to build a personal relationship with them, this book presents the identity of our Lord Jesus Christ to teenagers. Jesus Christ is our God and Savior. He is our friend, who cares about us, and leads us to a new and abundant life. We can help our students know Jesus Christ by adopting His message and His lifestyle, and living according to His Gospel. Living out these values means going counter culture, "Do not conform any longer to the pattern of this world, but be transformed by the renewing of your mind. Then you will be able to test and approve what God's will is; His good pleasing and perfect will" (Romans 12: 2). In this devotional journey, the participants will be encouraged to appreciate the choices of Jesus Christ and adopt real Christian values in their daily lives.

4. The Catechetical Dimensions

The catechesis is not an introduction to faith. It is a process by which we facilitate an intimate and personal encounter with the person of Jesus Christ. The main concern of the catechetical itinerary is not a theoretical knowledge of Christian faith, but rather a faith that is realized in daily human life within the community of believers. Therefore, the ultimate goal of any Christian educational itinerary should be to *announce the Good News of Jesus Christ as a source and fountain that provides sense to our human lives.*

Three focal points I intended to implement in writing this book. They are 1) the meaning of Christian living. 2) How can we live out our Christian faith in our real life. 3) How can we encourage the youth to be part of the community of believers.

4 .1. Christian Living

Christian living is the confluence of thoughts, emotions, and desires to form an integrated behavioral pattern and lifestyle. Living religiously is not enough. One must act and participate to his fullest ability just as Jesus did. To be a Christian is to participate in the life of Jesus. He who lives Christianity is already experiencing salvation and testing glory of the eternal life.

Christian living is realized, according to the Marcel Van Caster, through *three ascending levels* of individual development.

1. The first stage, which is *instruction,* has knowledge and understanding as its primary learning outcome. Therefore, while the learner can know and understand doctrine about God, he/she can never be said to know or understand God.

2. *Formation*: the second stage has values, attitudes, and feelings as its primary learning outcome. At this level the learner is helped out to reconstruct his values, his attitudes, and his feelings along Christian lines. Through this stage, the learner is helped to understand those crucial features of his/her self-understanding, or self-esteem, so often left untouched and undeveloped by the typical school or classroom. In this formation stage, the learner is helped to become more Christian by increasing his openness, not only to the gifts which God has freely bestowed upon him, but also to external activities in congruence with the divine life within him.

3. The third developmental stage is *initiation.* Its primary learning outcome is interpersonal communion, which, means the passage of the learner from the sector of a purely individual life to the life of fellowship both with his

> fellowmen and with God Himself. Through this interpersonal participatory life, Christians live fully the ongoing revelational experience, which is divine life in the world. God had fellowship with us through His Son Jesus Christ that we may know Him in a personal way and have an intimate fellowship with Him.

This curriculum endeavors to implement the three stages of Christian living Caster presents. With the assimilations, the stages of *instruction* to *doctrine*, and the *formation* to *morality* and the *initiation* to *community of believers*.

Through the pages of this study, students will discover the basic foundations of Christian doctrine (instruction), how to adopt and practice these elements in their daily life (formation), and the importance of community of believers, what is their role in it.

4.2. Rooted in our real life

Religious education is in itself life, not a preparation for life. Religion class is a laboratory and a workshop where students learn Christian living precisely by engaging in a here-and-now learning situation. Similar to what happens in the journey of the two disciples to Emmaus, the journey of religious education aims to challenge the learner to greet and meet God within him and God around him. From a pedagogical point of view, the most effective way of preparing a learner for the future is to help him live to the fullest a Christian life in the present, "I have come that they may have life, and have it to the full" (John 10: 10). The future, from one prospective, is the sum total of the individual's present.

In this curriculum, we explore the human experience of youth, their resources and potentiality, their difficulties and existential tasks. This curriculum also inspires a new understanding in life and encourages youth to discover their role in the life of the community.

4.3. Realized in Community

We also call educating the youth to be part of the community of believers a "socialization process." Socialization is that process by which a person is initiated into the life pattern that characterizes a particular group. An individual is socialized into a particular culture, or subculture, through his participation in the activities of certain agencies, including the family, peer group, the school and the parish.

A major focus of religious education is to consciously facilitate the socialization of an individual into the church community in particular, into the Christian fellowship community in general, and into God's intimate fellowship.

The last part of the book, *the Holy Church,* presents the life of the first Christian community. The church is recognized by its essential elements: loyalty to the Word of God, fraternal communion, the Holy Eucharist (Lord's supper) and prayer. The intent is to send an appeal to youth to feel and act as active members of the Body of Christ.

We find in the same unit the *ecumenical aspect of the Church*. Students will study, What is the ecumenical movements? what is the real ecumenism? In a pluralistic society and in an ecumenical age, socialization into the society of a particular Christian denomination is not sufficient. We ought to facilitate the individual's socialization into twin membership, first into his own particular Christian denomination and second into the community of Christendom as a whole. This issue is considered one of the most challenging aspects of religious education.

5. The Structure

Through the four units of the book, the student is invited to build a personal relationship with the Lord Jesus Christ. He is encouraged to enter the Church and become an active part of it.

1. Questioning Life

Life is a precious gift that God has given to us. The adolescent stage is compared to the season of spring in its flourish and vitality. Through the short notes, and through the questions for discussion, the partaker is directed in this first unit to look at himself and at the world around him. He will be encouraged to discover the work of the Holy Spirit in His creatures and the centrality of Jesus Christ in his personal and interpersonal life.

2. Listening to the Lord Who Speaks to us

God made promises to the patriarchs of the Old Testament and these promises have been fulfilled in the person of Jesus Christ. In the second unit, the students are encouraged to read the history of the people of the Old Testament as their own personal story. The purpose is to develop a Christian reading of the people and prophecies of the Old Testament.

3. Meeting Jesus Christ

The classes of the third unit have theological and personal goals: *the theological* is to teach students about Jesus Christ. He is the incarnated God, our Savior. *The personal* goal is to understand that the Savior Jesus Christ is our friend Who cares about us. He is our Lord Who guides and directs us to a new and abundant life. Therefore, the students are encouraged to build a personal relationship with our Lord. Such a relationship is based on friendship, love, honesty, and trust.

4. The Holy Church

Youth often feel rejected by adults within the church. Many of them do not have a sense of belonging to the community of believers. The Church is one body animated by the Holy Spirit; each one of us has a role in promoting the Church. The main purpose is to instruct students to understand the concept of the Church, and to develop a sense of belonging to the Body of Christ.

The Story of Emmaus

Now that same day, two of them were going to a village called Emmaus, about seven miles from Jerusalem. They were talking with each other about everything that had happened. As they talked and discussed these things with each other, Jesus himself came up and walked along with them, but they were kept from recognizing Him.

He asked them, "What are you discussing together as you walk along?"

They stood still, their faces downcast. One of them, named Cleopas, asked Him, "Are you only a visitor to Jerusalem and do not know the things that have happened there in these days?"

"What things?" He asked.

About Jesus of Nazareth they replied. "He was a prophet, powerful in word and deed before God and all the people. The chief priests and our rulers handed Him over to be sentenced to death and they crucified Him; but we had hoped that He was the One who was going to redeem Israel. And what is more, it is the third day since all this took place. In addition, some of our women amazed us. They went to the tomb early this morning but didn't find His body. They came and told us that they had seen a vision of angels who said He was alive. Then some of our companions went to the tomb and found it just as the women had said, but Him they did not see.

He said to them, "How foolish you are, and how slow of heart to believe all that the prophets have spoken! Did not the Christ have to suffer these things and then enter His glory?" And beginning with Moses and all the prophets, He explained to them what was said in all the Scriptures concerning Himself.

As they approached the village to which they were going, Jesus acted as if He were going farther. But they urged him strongly, "Stay with us, for it is nearly evening; the day is almost over." So He went in to stay with them.

When He was at the table with them, He took bread, gave thanks, broke it and began to give it to them. Then their eyes were opened and they recognize Him, and He disappeared from their sight. They asked each other "Were not our hearts burning within us while He talked with us on the road and opened the scripture to us?"

They got up and returned at once to Jerusalem. There they found the eleven and those with them, assembled together and saying, "It is true! The Lord has risen and has appeared to Simon. Then the two told what had happened on the way and how Jesus was recognized by them when He broke the bread

(Luke 24: 13 – 35, NIV)

The Courage of The Emmaus Journey

Cleopas and his friend accepted the invitation of Jesus Christ and followed Him, with enthusiasm, in the cities and villages of Palestine. Jesus talked about overcoming death, and about becoming the truth, the light, and the life. He preached to them about being the Good Shepherd who would lead the sheep to green pasture. He raised the dead man, and opened the eyes of the blind.

For three years, the disciples hoped that He would be the liberator that Israel had been waiting for. They hoped that Jesus would liberate them from the Romans, as Moses did when he liberated the Jews from the hand of Pharaoh. He promised them that they would become fishers of men, and they were waiting for the moment to embark upon their own spiritual journey.

However, their hope, joy, and happiness disappeared when they saw Jesus nailed to the Cross. They were shocked when they heard Him crying, "It is finished!" Everything was finished in an unexpected way! They lost hope that liberation would come again and they decided to return to their homes.

On their way to Emmaus, they were remembering, with bitterness, the lovely dream they had lived with Jesus. They were talking about their lives before and after they met with Him. Moreover, they were so sorry that the story of Jesus ended with the Crucifixion.

Suddenly, a man appeared from nowhere! He greeted them and started to talk to them, "You look very sad, what's going on with you my friends? Are you coming from a funeral?" Jesus asked.

The two disciples, not being able to recognize Jesus, were surprised that this man did not hear about the killing and the crucifixion that shook all Jerusalem, "Yes sir, indeed, we are coming from a funeral. Did you stay in Jerusalem on Friday? Did you hear about the killing of a preacher named Jesus? Yes, they killed Him and we were His followers.

We had hoped that He would restore the kingdom of Israel; however, he was killed before realizing that dream."

Cleopoas continues:

"Three days after His death Mary and some other women went to visit the tomb, but they found it empty! Nobody knows what happened to the body of Jesus. Some say He was resurrected, other say we, His disciples, stole the body; but we did not steal it.

We were afraid that they would kill us as they did to Jesus; therefore, we decided to go back to our village."

"And what do you think? What happened to Jesus?" the man asked the two disciples.

"We don't know sir. We are confused!" the two disciples replied.

The man started to talk with the disciples on their way to Emmaus. He walked with them all the way from Jerusalem to the village of Emmaus. They were talking about their lives, their sadness, and confusion. They were remembering what had happened to them when they were with Jesus before He died. They mentioned to Him their delusion when the Jews crucified Him.

The man tried to restore to them hope and joy. He explained to them from the Scriptures everything about Jesus' life, how the Jews were supposed to persecute Him, how He was suppose to die and be resurrected on the third day to save humanity.

Cleopas and his friend liked the way the man talked, the way He guided them and explained the Scriptures to them.

"So, then, we still have hope. He did not die for nothing, and they did not kill our joy. We have to look at the Scripture to understand that Jesus was supposed to die."

"Wait a second!" said the other disciple, "I now understand why, when we were approaching Jerusalem, Jesus talked about His glorification, and how He must be killed, and on the third day be raised to life."

"Do you also remember He mentioned the grain of wheat that unless it falls onto the ground and dies, it remains alone, but if it dies, it produces much grain?"

The conversation went on and on... and the two disciples began to understand how necessary the death and resurrection of Jesus was... He did not want to restore an earthly kingdom but rather an everlasting one.

The sunset began and they did not notice that they were almost home. They decided to invite the man to spend the night at their house, "Stay with us, for it is nearly evening; the day is almost over."

The man responded to their desires.

He entered the house, sat at the table,

He took the bread, lifted it up and blessed it,

"Take, eat, this is my Body, which is given for you."

Likewise, He took the cup, gave thanks, and handed it to them,

"This is the Blood of the New Covenant, which is shed for many, for the remission of sin."

Immediately after sharing the bread and wine with the man their eyes were opened and they recognized Him.

"It was the Lord, Jesus" Cleaopas said.

"Yes, and we did not recognize Him because we did not believe in what He said to us." His friend replied.

"We were blind and we now see. Let's go back to Jerusalem and tell the disciples what has happened to us."

*** *** *** *** ***

Our journey of faith is similar to that of the disciples of Emmaus. In our daily life, we get confused and worried; Jesus approaches us, speaks to us, and shares meals with us, that is His Body and Blood.

The journey that we are going to take in this book is similar to that of Emmaus: It is going to be divided into four stations.

1. QUESTIONING LIFE. The disciples of Emmaus were talking about their lives. They remembered with broken hearts the things that had happened to them while they were with Jesus Christ.

In the first station of our journey we will be encouraged by the readings and the group discussion to understand our daily lives that the Lord empowers with various experiences. Sometimes it is difficult to understand the real sense and meaning of these experiences. In these difficulties and ambiguities we must open our hearts to meet Jesus and walk with Him.

Ken Gire writes,

> Sometimes after entering into a relationship with Christ, we realize something else, that there is a difference between a personal relationship with Christ and an intimate one. In any relationship, it is the depth of the relationship that determines the depth of our conversations within the relationship. Our conversation, for example, with a stranger we are standing next to in the grocery store line is different from our conversations with someone we have met before, which is different from our conversations with a friend, which is different from our conversations with a close friend, which is different from our conversations with our best friend or with our mate.
>
> The same is true of our relationship with Jesus. Our level of intimacy within that relationship determines the depth of our conversations, both from us to Him and from Him to us (Ken Gire, *The reflective life,* Chariot Victor Publishing, Colorado Spring, Co 1998, p. 48.)

In this journey, we will be encouraged and instructed on how to build an intimate relationship with our Lord Jesus Christ. He is the center of our life, and He is the way, the truth and the life.

2. LISTENING TO THE LORD WHO SPEAKS TO US. "And beginning with Moses and all the prophets, He explained to them what was said in the Scriptures concerning Himself" (v. 27).

How do we listen to the Lord? The story tells us that Jesus explained from scripture about Himself. He meant the Old Testament because at that time, the New Testament was not yet written. The Old Testament was a preparation for the coming of our Lord Jesus Christ. God spoke to the people of the Old Testament about His coming through symbols and promises, and in the New Testament God spoke to us through the person of Jesus Christ.

This second station will explain to us how the experiences of the people of the Old Testament prepared for the coming of Jesus Christ. These experiences are ours; learning about them will help us answer our difficult questions and realize that our daily experiences are a place where God is close to us. In addition, through these experiences, God helps us to find meaning for our lives. Therefore, we listen to our Lord when we read and are in daily fellowship with His Word, the Bible.

3. MEETING JESUS CHRIST. Just as Jesus appeared to the disciples of Emmaus, and started to talk and discuss with them (v. 15), this station will help us discover who Jesus Christ is. He is God the Savior and our friend Who loves and cares about us.

4. ENTERING THE CHURCH. Jesus guided the disciples of Emmaus to enter the house, which is the symbol of the Church. He shared His Body and Blood with them (which are symbolized by the bread and wine) so they would recognize Him.

The last station will help us to understand what the Church is. Who forms the Church? How was the Church founded? What are the visible signs of the Church?

During this journey, we will also learn how to pray and how to be familiar with the Bible. Praying facilitates a relationship with our Lord. It also allows individuals to speak freely in confession about what may or may not be bothering them. We also need to be in a personal dialogue with the Lord to experience the Emmaus journey. The disciples of Emmaus during their journey talked freely with the Lord about their confusion and worry.

In this journey, we will meet many figures, and read many passages from the Bible. These readings will help us build a personal relationship with the Bible. The Bible is the only book that guides us in any journey of faith.

The journey that Jesus made with the disciples finished in *a celebration*. He blessed the food and shared it with them. The bread and wine are the two elements that we use to celebrate the Holy Eucharist. Our faith journey should always finish with the communion of His Blood and Body.

Ken Gire explains, in his book, *the Reflective Life*,

> Jesus comes to us in a thousand ways and for a thousand reasons, all of them for our good. "Behold," He says, "I stand at the door and knock; if anyone hears My voice and opens the door, I will come in to him, and will dine with him, and he with Me" (Revelation 3: 20). He comes knocking on the door of our heart, any time of the night or day, and to any of us who can recognize His voice through the thickness of the wood, He makes an amazing promise. He promises us a meal...
>
> It is a meal of mutual fellowship. I will dine with Him, and he with Me. It is also a meal of mutual nourishment. He will come to the door, however late He knocks, however lowly He appears in the doorway, it will be His presence that refreshes us and His words that nourish us (Ken Gire, p. 47).

Sharing a meal with Jesus signifies putting a portion of ourselves into that meal. Eating meal together is one of the most basic forms of giving and sharing. To invite Jesus to sit at your table, and break bread -as the disciples of Emmaus did- is to invite Him to share life with you.

Bread needs to be broken and shared. Bread broken and shared is life giving and nourishing, generous and Eucharistic. It already speaks of creation, of life and death, grain of wheat crushed, flour milled, bread made to sustain life.

I encourage you, dear friend, to start this journey. So, let's pray before we begin the walk.

In the name of the Father, the Son, and the Holy Spirit, One true God, to Whom be glory and upon us mercy and compassion forever and ever. Amen.

O Lord,

I'm here, together with my brothers and sisters,

ready to continue the journey that started two thousand years ago.

Many men and women, young and old;
many children and families,
in every part of the world,
are making this journey to You,
because You are the Lord of life and history.

We, as a community, are willing to receive Your Salvation,

We are ready to bring forth our contribution.

Dear Lord Jesus:

I will not get tired, or weary of serving Your plan of salvation.

I promise You Lord to keep in my mind,
the goals of the Emmaus journey. Amen.

Prophets of Hope Youth on a Mission

We are Prophets of hope, youth on a mission,
Spreading the Gospel of Christ.
We're prophets of hope, issuing the challenge:
To build the reign of God.

Pilgrims on a journey, marching towards our goal.
Led by the Spirit, strengthened by the Lord.
We bear each others burdens and give each other hope.
Following our Savior we press on towards our goals.

We come from towns and cities.
Laborers and students who want a better life,
We want to be successful, but not at any cost.
Unless we work for justice humanity is lost.

We face discrimination, poverty and drugs.
The values of our culture are all under attack.
But we have faith in Jesus; He will give us strength.
Together we will struggle to build a better world.

The Gospel is our map, the Church is our guide.
We're Christian youth who take a stand.
Leaders in our churches, reflecting as we go.
Learning from our set-backs, we never give up hope.

Adopted from,
Jose Antonio Rubio

First Station

GROWING IN LIFE TOGETHER

"They were talking to each other about everything that had happened" (Luke 24: 14).

Jesus asked, "What are you discussing together as you walk along? They stood still and their faces downcast" (Luke 24: 17).

1. A New Desire for Living

Shaun Martin, a sixteen year-old, wrote in his diary,

> Lately, I've started to wonder what it means when people say, "just be yourself!" It's a dumb thing to say to me right now because most of the time I'm not sure who I am! How can I be? I'm constantly changing. I mean, I look and sound totally different than I did just three months ago. Then I had a decent complexion; now it's oily and zit-ridden. Three months ago, my voice sounded like a normal human beings; now it fluctuates between squeaky one day and deep the next –like I'm echoing into a big drum or something. And some of my body parts look like they don't belong with other parts. I started working out last year, so I was really buffed. But I've grown five inches in the last six months, so I'm gangly and look completely out of proportion. I'm happy about getting taller, except that now my muscles don't look as big and my head looks as if it's sitting on a tall skinny post.
>
> I used to have no problem getting girls to come up and talk with me. Now I've lost confidence that they find me attractive. I worry that if by chance a girl should get interested, it'll only be a matter of time before she'll be turned off by my skin breaking out so much, or laugh when my voice does its squeak-and-croak act.
>
> It's not just my body that has changed –everything has. I've always thought of myself as a regular guy; but now, from one day to the next, my emotions are all over the place. One day, I feel up, the next down. Some days I think, "Hey, I'm really quite smart," and

> others, "I'm as dumb as a rock!" One week I'm sure what I want to do with my life, the next, I'm totally unsure. I'm a wreck! Really, I just want the real me to please stand up and stay around long enough for me to get used to him.

Shaun is not the only teenager who faces these kinds of physical and emotional changes. It is a change that every single teenager is experiences. Life is comprised of different seasons, stages and colors. Our teenage years are similar to spring with its liveliness and flourish. As new feelings grow in our lives we face new changes that sometimes make us run away and end up in some challenging circumstances. We feel that we do not have enough space to fulfill all the desires and aspirations inside us. We suffer a lot to gain wisdom, knowledge, inspiration, and friendship. In all of this, we learn one thing; we cannot reach anything in life without suffering.

Under these new changes, we experience the first delusions, the incomprehensible things that make us suffer, the loneliness that makes us bitter, the faults that throw us into disorder and make us worried about the future. In short, we can say that there is a new desire to face life in its many facets. We stand to question, experiment, ask, and evaluate everything. Many people think they can give us an answer to these questions only by offering information, but our need for relationships, friendships, and companionship is more important than just information.

All these desires and changes lead us to the first form of privacy, which is shown in dreams and diaries, and hiding ourselves in our room. In addition, these feelings are the signs of a maturing person.

But what is life?

The Holy Bible teaches us that human life is God's breath; a precious gift that God bestowed on us, and we are God's inspiration. We read in the book of Genesis, "The Lord God formed the man from the dust of the ground, and breathed into his nostrils the breath of life and the man became a living being" (Genesis 2: 7).

Not only that! The Bible tells us that God created us in His own Image, blessed us, and entitled us to rule and subdue the earth,

"So God created man in His own image
in the image of God, He created him,
male and female He created them.
God blessed them and said to them,
"Be fruitful and increase in number;
Fill the earth and subdue it.
Rule over the fish of the sea and the bird of the earth,
and over every living creature that moves on the ground"(Genesis 1: 27– 28).

This passage from the book of Genesis teaches us that God blessed us and asked us to subdue the earth, and rule over it. We should, therefore, feel a great sense of power, self acceptance and responsibility when we learn that we are created in God's image and for God's purpose.

Moreover, the story of creation tells us that God anointed man with a mission, "The Lord God took the man and put him in the Garden of Eden to work it and take care of it" (Genesis 2: 15).

After bestowing the precious gift of life and empowering him to rule over the earth, God asked man to work and take care of the world around him. He commanded man to do his best to promote human life and make it more meaningful and successful.

We should feel a great sense of power, self acceptance and responsibility when we learn that we are created in God's image and for God's purpose.

When do we receive these gifts?

We receive this anointing when you confess with your mouth and believe in our heart that Jesus is your personal

Lord and Savior, He died on the Cross on your behalf, He rose again (read, Romans 10: 9-10). When your mouth and heart believe and confess this truth, God, through His Holy Spirit, gives you power to be His Son (read John 1: 12-13).

The book of Revelation declares that Jesus Christ loved us and gave his life (blood) that we may have such power and authority, "to Him Who loved us and washed us from our sins in His own blood, *and has made us kings and priests* to His God and Father, to Him be glory and dominion forever and ever. Amen" (Revelation 1: 6).

Dear friend,

God has anointed you since you were born to be part of His kingdom, you became a king/queen over this earth. The devil tries always to fumble that crown you have received; the devil, who the Bible calls "deceitful", seeks to make you a slave to sin; his intention is always to make you feel bad about yourself, not accepting yourself as God's image.

You may be struggling with a bad habit, or poor self-image, or sin that you cannot overcome, or anything that makes you feel a slave, or any thoughts that prevent you from thinking and acting as a king or queen, as a ruler over the earth, over the fish in the sea, and the birds of the air, and over every living creature that moves on the ground. No matter what your struggles or challenges are, God has a purpose for you which is to renew the gift, the power, and the anointing that you received in the day you confessed Him as your Lord and Savior and were Baptized in the name of the Father the Son and the Holy Spirit.

Every time you feel bad about yourself and suffer a poor self image, stand in front of the mirror and repeat the anointing that God has empowered you. Read aloud the same verses from the book of Genesis: "Be fruitful and increase in number; Fill the earth and subdue it. Rule over the fish of the sea and the birds of the air, and over every living creature that moves on the ground." And God will grant you victory over the weaknesses that you have.

Discuss with your friends

- What kind of thoughts come to your mind when you look at your image in a mirror?
- What is life?
- What are the positive and negative aspects of your life?

2. Difficult Questions

At this age you may tend to be suspicious of your previous religious experience while you face new experiences, changes, and feelings. You may have the desire and tendencies to abandon your religious beliefs. Sometimes, abandoning religion is the result of non-commitment or the result of being far from the Church. This abandonment may disturb you. You may feel as if you are loosing a reference point and an encouraging part of your life.

Also, in this stage of your life, you ask many difficult questions such as, what is the meaning of life, death, love, and suffering; is it significant to believe in God, or not? These questions increase as we enlarge our experiences.

Faith becomes constricting like tight clothing when confronted with your larger horizon of experiences. Many times you think that the religious world is weak and religion has not developed enough to answer all the questions in your life. Many times you stand to ask, "is faith worthwhile in my life?".

All these difficult questions you face in your life mark the existence of every single person and community. Even in ancient times, man tried to answer these questions and developed many proverbs and words of wisdom to understand the world around him. Throughout history this quest followed one of three paths,

1. *Philosophy*, man tried to find answers in his intellect and rationality.
2. *Mysticism*, man tried to find answers in his feelings and emotions.
3. *Morality*, man tried to find answer in the self-control and discipline.

The bible teaches us that all these attempts failed, because man is born,

1. Spiritually blind, (read, 2 Corinthians 4: 1-4; 1 Corinthians 2: 14)
2. Spiritually dead (read, Ephesians 2: 1-5)
3. An Enemy of God, (read Romans 5: 6-10)

Any successful and fulfilling answer must come from outside of man, it must come from God Himself. There is no real answer to the basic questions of life apart from God. That is why God has spoken to man in His Word.

From the people of the Old Testament we have learned that God Himself speaks through all events and experiences that circulate our planet. The Bible presents the fruit of these witnesses, especially in the Wisdom Books in the Old Testament; for example, the book of Job, Proverbs, and Ecclesiastes. In these books, God teaches us how to read the events of our lives and interpret them.

The wise men of the Old Testament, under the guidance of the Holy Spirit, have answered the fundamental questions of life, such as how to live a happy and peaceful life and why does suffering and pain exist. The Bible guides you to learn by observing the world and reflecting on your experiences.

From Psalm 37
Trust in the Lord and do good;
Dwell in the land and enjoy safe pasture.
Delight yourself in the Lord
And He will give you the desire of your heart

Discuss with your Friends

- How do you feel when you hear words like "Religion," "God," and "Church"?
- What are the most important questions you face? Would you want a clear answer to them?
- Who is the person who can help you in your difficult researches and questions?

3. Jesus Christ is the Center of Our Lives

We can have answers to all our questions and difficult issues in our meeting with the person of Jesus Christ. Our entire life and expectations should center in the person of Jesus Christ. This was the experience of the first disciples of Christ who, after the resurrection, and under the guidance of the Holy Spirit, were made open to faith in Jesus. Their lives were enlightened with a new and significant meaning, "When the day of Pentecost came, they were all together in one place. Suddenly a sound like the blowing of violent wind came from heaven and filled the whole house where they were sitting. They saw what seemed to be tongues of fire that separated and came to rest on each of them. All of them were filled with the Holy Spirit and began to speak in other tongues as the Spirit enabled them" (Acts, 2: 1 – 4).

The disciples walked the entire journey with Jesus; they followed Him for three years learning how to grow in faith. Nevertheless, before Jesus was lifted up to heaven, He promised them to send the Holy Spirit that would stay with them, teaching them everything.

The disciples discovered a new sense of direction for their lives when they received the Holy Spirit. They were born again through the Holy Spirit as the Bible describes it,

"Yet to all who received Him, to those who believed in His name, He gave the right to become children of God, children born not of natural descent, nor of human decision of husband's will, but born of God" (John, 1: 12 – 13).

"...For you have been born again not of perishable seed, but imperishable, through the living and enduring Word of God" (1 Peter 1: 23).

We also, as the first disciples of Jesus, must be guided by the Holy Spirit. Some of us have been confirmed in our churches; confirmation symbolizes receiving the Holy Spirit. However you have to understand that these practices will not save you. We need faith and grace. Our sanctification is made possible by faith in Jesus Christ through His Grace. The sacraments are the means by which we receive the Grace of God. They are the visible signs through which we show and declare our faith in Jesus Christ. Without the power of the Holy Spirit and the Grace of God our efforts for sanctification are worthless.

You may ask, what is faith?

Faith in people is a kind of trust or confidence, a willingness to depend on them. We have faith in different people and, depending on who and what they are, our faith has different nuances. For example, we have faith in doctors, mechanics, and politicians. Some of these matters are of more importance than others. Religious faith is trust or dependence of a deeper kind. It is a trust in someone in relation to the most profound questions and concerns of life. Questions such as: Who am I? Where did I come from? What is my ultimate meaning? Is there some kind of deity that made me? What kind? Is It benign or hostile, interested or uninterested? Can I be in contact with It? Does my salvation or fulfillment relate to it? Why do I have to die? Is there life after death? These are questions of ultimate concern.

We find that the New Testament message speaks to just such great areas. It is a message about God and His nature, about his initiative in our regard, about our meaning and destiny, about the centrality of Jesus Christ in world history, about love and mercy, about hope for a kingdom. The acceptance of the great Christian stories, if it is a genuine acceptance, gives our lives their fundamental character and direction. It shapes our understanding and vision, our sense of ourselves and our world, our meanings, our hopes, fears and aspirations. It informs our consciousness, affection and loyalties.

To understand these notes, I invite you to read the following faith journey of a young man like you.

Like many children in this melting pot called "America," I grew up in a culturally mixed family. From my mother, I received a Jewish heritage, although, this was more of a cultural connection than it was one of religious practice. Her side of the family did not faithfully adhere to the majority of the Jewish rites and rituals. As a matter of fact, the kosher laws were about all they observed regarding the faith. In addition, my mom grew up with a mother who taught her to believe that Jesus was the Messiah. So, in a sense, Mom was a Messianic Jew.

My father grew up in a very orthodox, pre-Vatican II Catholic[2] family who faithfully adhered to the teaching, doctrine, practices, and obligation of the Church. Because my mother believed in Jesus, she and Dad had no qualms about having me baptized in the Catholic faith and training me up to it.

As a young child, several experiences impressed the reality of God on my fresh mind and heart, although it obviously takes hindsight to see God's movement in my toddler, and early child years. I remember being given the opportunity as a family to bring the gifts to the altar during the offertory at Mass one Sunday. The usher placed in my hands what would become the Body of Christ and told me to "take care of it." I remember feeling a sense of awe, although I really did not understand why at the time. I remember to this day (word for word) the bedtime prayers my mom and dad would say with me every night which included a spoken blessing on every one of my immediate and extended family, including the pets!

2 The Second Vatican Council was held between 1964–1968, in the Vatican City. In it, the Catholic Church reformed much of its theology and doctrine. Pre-Vatican means conservative.

Family prayer was also an upheld tradition before dinner and during special seasons such as Lent and Advent.

As a child, I even contemplated (as do most boys) becoming a priest and would go so far as to play "Mass" with my sister. I would be the priest, she would be my congregation, and Wonder Bread would be our nourishment.

When I hit my junior high and early high school years and began to think more critically, there was a brief interlude where the call to Christianity became somewhat tainted and misconceived by natural developmental issues as well as my observation of "the church" around me.

The Church did not seem all that exciting or relevant to me. I briefly questioned the legitimacy of the Christian life. I did not necessarily pursue rebelling against the Church or the faith foundation my parents helped to establish in my life. I just wanted something real.

As a part of my Confirmation preparation, I was required to attend an overnight retreat. On this retreat, young adults shared with me through skits, talks, and other activities what Jesus Christ meant to them. They gave me an impression of Jesus unlike any that I ever had before. They spoke as if they knew Him personally (they showed me something real), and for the first time in my life I began to understand that Jesus wanted to be a part of my life twenty-four hours a day, seven days a week, 365 days a year. He did not simply want to be put in a compartment called "Sunday Mass" or "youth group."

During my final two years in high school, I served as a peer minister at my parish, and discerned God's call for me to take Jesus' message to teens through youth ministry as my life's vocation.

I love Jesus Christ. As I look on my life, I can see His protective, firm, loving, and providential hand guiding me into a relationship with Him through the influence of countless people, experiences, and events. My walk with Jesus did not begin as did the Apostle Paul's with a radical 180 degree about-face, but rather like his disciple Timothy's through a gradual process of growing and learning, a process that will span my entire life.

Discuss with your Friends

- What place does Jesus Christ have in your life?
- Do you have any group or place where you share your friendship with the person of Jesus Christ?

Prayer of Awaking

Awaken us, Lord, from our sleep of sin,
That we may praise Your watchfulness.
You Who watch and do not sleep;
give life to our death in the sleep of death and corruption,
that we may give thanks for Your compassion,
You who live and do not die;
grant us in the glorious company of the angels,
that we may praise You and bless You in holiness,
because You are praised and blessed in heaven and on earth,
Father, Son and Holy Spirit, now and always and forever.

4. To Learn to Grow Up with Others

Each one of us builds his own way of life through the facts and experiences that the world offers him, the family in which we grow, the country in which we live, the friends with whom we interact and the school in which we study. All these elements shape our personality and life. Nobody lives on an isolated island. The plant of life does not grow in an isolated desert, but in connection with the world where we live and grow.

The Family

The first environment that shapes our lives is the family. Living in a family day after day we create strong bonds that leave their marks on our lives. Through daily contact with family members, we learn the alphabet of communication with others, and we learn how to love each other.

During this adolescent stage, you demonstrate a desire for independence and look for a new kind of relationship with your parents, brothers, and sisters. You might face obstacles in connecting with them because of your tendencies to be different from them.

As teenagers, some of your biggest challenges are with your parents. You are beginning to separate from them and become more independent. This is difficult for you and for them. You are also at an age when you begin to have different opinions, different priorities, and different lifestyles. It is okay to have these feelings. It does not mean you don't love your parents; it is just part of growing up.

Questions for reflection

- How do you see your relationship with your family?
- What obstacles do you face in connecting with your family?

Friends

Besides family, there are friends. Meeting places like malls, parks, and fast food restaurants are enough to create the world of friendship. After a long day at school, companionship with schoolmates can be a way we can relax and enjoy our time. We can spend hours and hours talking and passing time. We can also stay together to develop our own identity, our own projects and aspirations.

However, it is also necessary to distinguish between destructive and constructive friendships. The Bible says,

"A friend loves at all times and a brother is born for adversity" (Proverbs 17: 17).

"There is a friend who sticks closer than a brother" (Proverbs 18: 24).

In your daily activities at school you meet different kinds of friends. They come from different ethnic, religious, and social backgrounds. You should learn how to distinguish between the friends who can help you grow in your Christian life, and the people that compromise your Christian beliefs.

There is a similar picture in the first twelve verses of the third chapter of the book of Daniel. I invite you to open your Bible to the book of Daniel and read this passage.

Read Daniel 3: 1 – 12

The Old Testament records the story of Daniel and his three friends who were persuaded to compromise their faith, and bow down to the golden image that Nebuchadnezzar had built. It was made of gold and stood 900 feet high. It was placed out on the plain, so that it could be seen for miles as the golden image of the king. Daniel's account reveals that thousands of people gathered on the plain of Dura. The dedication program was planned. As the orchestra began to play, all of the people were to bow down and worship the image of Nebuchadnezzar. Those who would not do so would meet a terrible fate. They would be thrown into Babylon's burning fiery furnace. It was at this very point that the faith of these Hebrew men met their greatest test. Should they go along with the crowd, just this time? After all, they could get lost in this great multitude of people and bow down along with them and hardly anyone would notice. Or should they stand out like a sore thumb, remain faithful to their convictions, and not bow down to the golden image? This test of faith eventually finds its way to all of us in some way.

The account of Daniel and his friends is a very intriguing picture. It is woven throughout what we would call today "peer pressure." There are a lot of young people in our contemporary culture out on the plain of Dura. They have bought into the teaching that tells them they will not be popular unless they go along with the crowd, unless they bow down with others. After all, they are convinced that everyone else is doing it so why not go ahead and bow down.

In the beginning of the story, we read that Daniel and his friends "resolved, or purposed, in their hearts not to defile themselves" (Paraphrased, Daniel 1: 8). These young men are not speaking softly in these verses; they are passionate; they are saying, "Don't give in, and be resistant." They drew the line when it comes to the Word of God. This is the point at which they resisted. They didn't give into the peer pressure around them; they made some tough decisions.

We are living in modern Babylon. We are faced with the same challenge that Daniel and his friends faced more than 2000 years ago. However, Daniel did not give in, he was consistent. You ought to be the Daniel of your school, family and society.

One of the reasons so many of us fall into our own world is that we do not know what the Bible's teachings say, and, thus, we compromise and assimilate ourselves into the culture with no real convictions. Seldom do we "resolve and purpose in our hearts" so that when the time comes and we have to make a decision, we've already made it in our hearts and minds.

The young men in the book of Daniel were just teenagers like you at that time. Most of life's major decisions are made in our youth. Decisions regarding our careers, our marriage, our friends, our habits, even decisions of trusting Christ are made when we are young. Daniel made his decision long before he got to Babylon. He "purposed in his heart" to stand upon the Word of God. Daniel did not wait until he got to an intersection of life to decide which way he would turn. He had already made his mind up before he got there.

What are the criteria we should use in our culture today to determine which activities we should engage in and which we should not? Some would say peer pressure. For Daniel it was the Word of God; he set his mind and he purposed in his heart. Life is full of intersections, and "compromise" is the name of the game in our culture today. Daniel is saying to us across the centuries, "Don't give in, be resistant".

There are always two ways to respond when we feel

peer pressure. If we are controlled by the Word of God and the teachings of the Church, we will respond with conviction. If we are controlled by the world we will respond with compromise.

Many are prone to give up what they stand for when they're out in the world. Some of us seem to think that if we do not compromise we might lose our position or even our popularity. Daniel had figured out who he wanted on his side. He knew the truth of Proverbs 16: 7, "When a man's ways please the Lord, He makes even his enemies to be at peace with him."

We should live our lives in such a way that they line up with the Word of God and please Him in the process. And then we can watch Him work on those around us as He did in Daniel's day. It is not enough to simply be resistant if we are not consistent. Some start well but give up and go with the crowd around them.

So, what is the point? If we are going somewhere in life we need to learn lessons and advice from the people that are presented in the Bible. There are many other people, like Daniel, in the Bible that encourage us in our faith journey.

To understand more of what I have said, let's read the testimony of this young man.

> Although I grew up in a Catholic home with wonderful parents and a good support system, my commitment to my faith came through a "Paul" type of experience. During my college years at a Jesuit University, I all but left the Catholic Church. It was during this time that I began to participate in many deviant behaviors that lead to much pain and disillusionment. I transferred to the school halfway through a semester; everyone seemed to already be in their own group, and I desperately wanted to fit in. A few guys invited me to go "out for a beer" and I slowly began to drink regularly. The following school year, I whole-heatedly began a lifestyle of loose living and partying. I began participating in activities that only a few years earlier, I despised.

Toward the end of my junior year, with poor grades, poor dating relationships, and not a very good relationship with my parents, I decided it was time to straighten up. Instead of living with five other guys, it was time to move in with someone that was more focused on graduating. I found an engineering student to room with for my senior year, the only guy from our dorm floor that didn't drink.

I returned from summer break with a resolve to stay away from the bar scene and study daily. I even worked on a few *"I will..."* statements such as: "I will study every evening for at least two hours," and "I will consume only what is good for my body." It seemed to be working... for about the first week, anyway. I stopped by my buddies' place and they were all sitting around getting high... and I joined in. For the next month, I lived with wanting to follow through with my commitments, but not having the willpower. Around mid-term when grades came out I was at my lowest point ever- angry and frustrated with my self, not to mention pulling a couple of D's.

I remember calling home and talking with my mom about this time. I expressed that she just would not believe the things I had gotten into during college and it was a very difficult time. Then she said, "Ever since you've been going to school up there, you have turned away from God and become a different person." I knew she was right, but I really did not think God could help me.

A week or so later, I went with seven friends to a Van Halen concert. As we arrived, I mentioned to a friend that I was bummed we were so far back and that I had forgotten my glasses. Nevertheless, we were having a great time jamming along on our air guitars. About halfway through the concert, I started thinking to myself, "I have so much... a good education, a good family, lots of friends, a cool VW bus, and lots of other things. If I have so much then why do I feel so empty inside?" Then Van Halen began to play a song called "Best of Both Worlds."

The song begins, "I don't know what I'm living on, but it's not enough to fill me up." I could not believe my ears, they felt the same way I did! The song goes on to say, "we want the best of both worlds." I thought to myself that's like me. I want to party and to do whatever I want and in the end I hope to go to heaven. The song continues, "You don't have to die and go to heaven or hang around to be born again." At that moment it hit me: is it possible we are both missing the same thing... God? Then I immediately felt a voice in my head say: "Do you see the sweat on Sammy Hagar's face and read their t-shirt and banner. I started to tear up and Chris said: "What's going on with you?" I responded "I'm OK, this is a great concert."

That evening I dropped my friends off at the bar and went home. I took a few jeers for it. When I got back to my apartment, I dusted off my Bible and got down on my knees. "God," I prayed, "If You are real and what happened tonight was real, I want to know it". I spent the next few hours, until early in the morning, crying and repenting for all I had done, reading Scripture through the eyes of faith, and asking God into my life. The Lord revealed Himself to me in a wonderful way. My life changed drastically! What I could not accomplish with "I will" statements, God accomplished in me through His power! My addictions were gone immediately. I stopped going to bars. I started going back to Mass and spent time daily with the Lord. I got involved in a senior retreat and Bible study. I individually shared what God had done in my life with many of my partying friends. One commented that he thought I was maybe a prophet sent from God.

Since that time, the Lord has called me to full-time youth ministry to share the love that He

> shared with me. I have been blessed with a beautiful Christian wife and two wonderful daughters. The Lord has taken care of my every need and I truly want nothing. The meaning, purpose, and belonging I hungered for I found in Christ and His Church.

What do we learn from this testimony? It is the story of every single one of us. It is a story of the challenges that we face in our daily life. He was in Babylon and he joined the crowd, but was repentant later.

At the beginning of his journey this young man responded to the world and he compromised and failed. But when he turned to the Word of God, the Grace of God empowered him, his faith grow stronger and stronger and he lived by conviction.

Beliefs alone aren't enough to make us stand strong for Christ. You also need conviction. Beliefs are in your head. With enough pressure they can be swayed, challenged, even changed! But convictions are cemented in your heart and no trial is able to dislodge them.

Being bold for Christ is risky. Stand up for Christ today by saying no to temptation, to cheating, refusing to join the crowd in wrong activities; sharing your faith in Christ with your friends; taking your Bible to school; inviting others to church or a youth group function.

Work it out

What do you purpose in your heart?

Sit down and write out your true convictions, those things you feel the strongest about, those principles you are committed to no matter what the cost or risk.

If you don't have convictions, or if you have very few, ask God to turn your beliefs into convictions: Ask Him to give you the resolve and commitment of Daniel. Tell Him you want to have an influence in your school and in your neighborhood.

The Opposite Sex

During adolescence, we begin to discover our own bodies, the physical and psychological structure of men and women. We experience the first feelings of attraction to the opposite sex. We become interested in entering the world of the other, to know their physical aspects, sensibilities, and spiritual qualities that sometimes are different from our own. We learn also that being different from others is not a bad thing, it is enriching. Our network of communication will enlarge when we connect with others. Sometimes we face difficulties in connecting with the opposite sex so we find ourselves caged in wrong and unreal fantasies. We look for a distorted sexuality that the media (television, internet, etc.) offers us. In this way, we look to the opposite sex as an object of satisfaction, not as a person to share our experiences, projects, and aspirations with.

In our adolescent years we want so much to be loved, to be cared for, to be genuine, to be authentic, and to be accepted. You feel you should develop friendship skills, but that takes time, so you give in to the instant access to follow peer pressure and engage in sexual behavior.

The biggest temptation is to see yourself as a victim, and you end up lamenting your fate. Lamenting your fate is the opposite of honoring the struggle. Lamenting your fate means willingly participating in being a victim and making it seem like, “everything is all right.”

Many of our teenage friends are looking for love. Because they are inexperienced, they give in to dreams and fantasies that lead them to see it where it does not yet exist. The desire to fall in love gives birth to passion and gleaming vision. We do not want to miss the chance for love, so we take high risks and lose often.

Sexuality is extraordinary richness. It may become a constructive factor in our lives if we know how to direct it. However, giving in to wrong sexual behavior harms spiritual growth. Whatever impedes union with God and union with others harms spiritual growth.

Remember what we learned from the story of Daniel

and his friends. I want to remind you of it again, and tell you more about it.

When we hear the name Daniel some of us think of an out of-date-prophet. Some have the idea that he was some old guy with no idea of what it's like to live in a culture like ours with our struggles and challenges. Not at all! Daniel was a real guy, living in a real world with real problems. He had a real job in the real marketplace. He was surrounded by real men and women in his office who were hostile to his belief system and his faith. They had their "new age" application to life. In fact, in the fifth chapter of the book we find him at a real office party with alcohol and women everywhere.

The story of Daniel is the story of a young man who understood our challenges. It is the story of someone who was confronted with the same difficulties and hard decisions that we are called upon to make every day. He was plopped down in a culture that pressured him to stuff his religious roots way back in the corner of the office closet. He found himself in a world that tempted him to take the easy way to the top. Yet, his is a story that offers help and hope.

The first chapter of Daniel concludes, "Thus Daniel *remained [continued]* until the first years of King Cyrus" (Daniel 1: 21). Daniel and his friends passed all tests, and God gave them knowledge in all matters of wisdom and understanding. Yes! Daniel "remained" or "continued," as The New King James Version translates it. He continued and remained faithful to God's Word and he continued to resist the pressure around him. Therefore, God gave Daniel and his friends protection, wisdom, and influence along the way. This should be a tremendous encouragement for all of us. It would be wonderful if it were said of us that we too "continued." That we did not give in, nor give up, nor give out. That we too were resistant, consistent, and persistent.

Questions for reflection

- Do you have any adult you freely talk to about your intimate life?

- Is a relationship with your friend (female/male) based on mutual respect or not?

Concluding this chapter, I would like to remind you of what we have learned in the first point of this chapter. God has created you and put you in this earth to work it and take care of it. The Lord has anointed you and blessed you to be fruitful and rule over every living creature that moves on the ground.

Being with others is a fundamental aspect to our growth. It is not possible to fulfill our projects and aspirations without connecting and caring for the world and the environment around us.

How do you pray

In the name of the Father, the Son, and the Holy Spirit, One true God, to Whom be glory and upon us mercy and compassion forever and ever. Amen.

Holy, Holy, Holy, Lord God Almighty.
Heaven and earth are full of Your glory.
Hosanna in the highest.
Blessed is He Who has come, and is to come in the name of the Lord God; Praise be in the highest.

Holy are You, o God
Holy are You, the Almighty
Holy are You Immortal Who were crucified for us: have mercy upon us.

Lord, have mercy upon us.
Lord, have pity and mercy upon us.
Lord, accept our service and our prayers,
and have mercy upon us.
Glory to You, o God.
Glory to You, Creator.
Glory to You, Christ the King, Who has compassion on Your sinful servants. Amen.

Pray with Psalm

O Lord, our Lord
how majestic is Your name in all the earth.

When I consider Your heavens the work of Your fingers,
the moon and the stars which You have set in place,

What is man that You are mindful of him,
the son of man that You care for him?

You made him a little lower than the heavenly beings
and crowned him with glory and honor.

You made him ruler over the works of Your hands;
You put everything under his feet.

Second Station

LISTENING TO THE LORD WHO SPEAKS TO US

"And beginning with Moses and all the prophets, He explained to them what was said in all the Scriptures concerning himself" (Luke 24: 27).

The Scriptures the Word of God to Us

"And then beginning with Moses and all the prophets, He explained to them what was said in all Scriptures concerning Himself" (Luke 24: 27).

Jesus Christ started to talk with the disciples of Emmaus about what Moses and the Prophets said about Him. To learn about Jesus Christ and develop a relationship with Him we should read the Holy Scriptures, to discover who Jesus Christ is and what His message is for us.

Before discovering what the Scriptures say about Jesus, we have to ask what we mean by Scriptures. When we say Scriptures we mean the Bible. The Bible contains writings recorded over a period of two thousand years. It started about 1850 B.C. till 100 A.D. Through the events and experiences of the Bible, we see the unfolding of the great event: the story of salvation that God intended to be realized for humanity. The center of this story is Jesus Christ, His death and resurrection. Through the events and persons of the Bible, God makes a journey with His people. Through symbols, He revealed Himself to the fathers of the Old Testament, Abraham, Isaac, Jacob, Moses, and all the prophets. Finally, He revealed Himself in Jesus Christ, Who is the Word of God Who became flesh. This manifestation, or revelation, comes to us gradually. That is the reason we have two Testaments, the New and the Old. The Old Testament, in 46 books, tells us the history of the

Jewish people from Abraham and his descendent up to the coming of Jesus Christ. The New Testament, in 26 books, tells us the experiences of the first Christian community from the birth of Jesus Christ until the end of the first century. It is divided into the following parts: The four Gospels: Matthew, Mark, Luke, and John, the Acts of the Apostles, the Apostolic letters which are: St. Paul's (14 letters), St. James' (1 letter), St. Peter's (2 letters), St. John's (2 letters), St. Judas (1 letter), and the Revelation of John.

The Bible in our Christian Life

There are a few important aspects you have to consider before reading the Bible:

1. The Bible explains to us how God loved us and saved us from our sins, "For God so loved the world that He gave His one and only Son that whoever believes in Him shall not perish" (John 3: 16).
2. All the books of the Bible were written under the guidance of the Holy Spirit. He is the real author of the Holy Scripture. St. Paul says: "All Scripture is God-breathed" (2Timothy 3:16). God so supernaturally directed the writers of Scripture without waving their human intelligence, literary style, or personal feelings. His complete and coherent message to man was recorded with perfect accuracy, the very words of the original Scripture bearing the authority of Divine authorship.
3. The Bible is *an alliance & experience between God and man*. This experience started in the past and it still continues today in the Church.
4. The Bible is also *a seed*. If we read the Bible with faith, the seed will grow in our hearts and become a message of life, hope, and happiness. That is what Jesus taught us in the parable of

the sower. Jesus compares the Word of God to a seed that, when it falls into the good soil and grows, produces crops (turn to Luke 8: 4 – 18). St. Paul advised his disciple Timothy saying, "...from your infancy you have known the Holy Scriptures, which are able to make you wise for salvation through faith in Christ Jesus. All Scripture is God-breathed and is useful for teaching, rebuking, correcting and training in righteousness, So that the man of God may be thoroughly equipped for every good work" (2 Timothy 3: 15 – 17).

Let us pray before starting this station.

Grant us, O Lord God, the knowledge of Your divine words,
and fill us with understanding of Your Holy Gospel,
the richness of Your divine gifts, and that of Your Holy Spirit.
Grant us that, with joy, we may keep Your commandments,
perform and fulfill Your will,
and become worthy of Your blessings and mercies,
our Lord and our God now and forever. Amen

Attention In this second station of our journey, we will meet some people from the Old Testament, we will learn lessons for our Christian life, and we will learn how the events of the Old Testament were preparing for the coming of our Lord Jesus Christ.

Studying the Bible

If we are Christians, it makes sense that you'd want to learn as much as you could about Jesus Christ and His word. You can do that by talking about the Bible with your friends and family, writing down verses or memorizing them. You can also learn by going to church and listening to what your pastor or youth leader says.

Think about it –of all the things you learn in your life what's the most important? It's not algebra or biology! Although studying these subjects is important and necessary, **the most important thing is to know who God is and what He wants you to do in your life.** And the more you learn about Him, the more you feel secure and have strength for whatever challenges you have to face. Reading the Bible is the best kind of studying.

Being better witness

I had some friends who weren't Christians, but I had no idea how to witness to them. I hadn't really studied the Bible, and I didn't understand how important it was for me to show my faith through my life.

Those old friends are lost. They are caught up in swearing, sex, drugs and whatever else they can find to fill the emptiness of not having Jesus in their lives. I know it's not my fault that they are doing these things, but if I had known the Bible better a few years ago, at least I could have tried to help them know Jesus. It is really important that we take time to study God's Word and know it. Then we can be better witnesses to our friends.

Discuss with your friends

- Who is the real author of the Bible?
- Think of a time that you really enjoyed reading the Bible. What made you so excited about it?
- If someone asked you a tough question about the Bible, would you know how to find the answer?
- How can you be better prepared to talk with your non-Christian friends about Jesus?

Meditating on God's Word

Father,

I know that when I am meditating on Your Word that there is a work being done on within me.

For only Your Word which is alive, and actively at work in me, has the ability to expose the truth about myself.

Only Your Word hidden in my heart has the power to change and transform me into the image of Christ.

I will always give attention to Your Word and will not let It depart from before my eyes.

I will meditate upon it in my heart for it is truly life to me and health to my entire body.

I will meditate upon Your Word day and night and I will never stop speaking Your Word knowing that It will make my life successful and all my ways prosperous.

Father,

My desire is that when the storms, trials and pressures of life come, that my heart would be so full of Your Word and faith that It would flow out of me like a river and sustain me through all the difficulties of life.

Your Word shall be a lamp unto my feet and a light unto my path. It makes the way plain before me.

I am diligent to study Your Word and eager to present myself to You as a servant who has no cause to be ashamed.

One who accurately understands and applies the Word of truth.

I so desire to do Your Will.

Just as the rain and snow are sent from heaven to earth to accomplish a purpose, so is Your Word. It shall not return to You void but will bear fruit and accomplish what You desire.

I know that when I speak Your Word I am sending It back to you, believing that It will succeed in the matter for which It is being sent.

Lord,

You sustain all things by Your powerful Word, which You have exalted above all.

Help me to hold fast to my confession of hope without wavering, for You Who promised are faithful.

I know that I shall declare a thing and it will be established for me so that Your light will shine upon me.

I will speak Your Word to the mountain and I will not doubt in my heart but will believe that those things that I speak shall be done. Amen.

1. Adam and Eve

Attention In the next points of our journey, we are going to talk about our old fathers in faith and the promises God made to them. We will meet those fathers through the reading of some stories presented in the first book of the Bible, the book of Genesis. Genesis is a Greek word meaning "origin", "source", or "generation". It was given this name because it tells us about the origin of the world and man.

In this phase, I want you to take your Bible, open it and read the stories that I have indicated to you. In this way, you will become more familiar with the use of the Bible.

Christians believe that Adam and Eve are the first man and woman God created. He made Adam from the dust of the earth and placed him in the Garden of Eden. God knew man's need to be with others of his kind, so He formed the woman, Eve using Adam's rib. After creating Adam and Eve, God gave them the task to work in the Garden and to take care of it (Read Genesis 2: 7 – 24).

God told Adam that he could eat from every tree in the Garden except from the tree of knowledge of good and evil. One day, as Eve was walking alone in the garden, the serpent questioned her concerning God's command. Eve explained they could eat from all trees except one. Satan tempted Eve assuring her that she and Adam would not die, but they would be like God knowing good and evil.

Eve disobeyed God's command and ate the fruit; also, she gave it to Adam. Having their eyes opened, Adam and Eve knew they were naked and tried to cover themselves with fig leaves.

God came into the Garden seeking Adam and Eve, but

they hid because they knew they had disobeyed God. As God questioned them about their sin, Adam blamed Eve and Eve blamed the serpent. God punished Adam and Eve for their disobedience and rebellion by sending them out of the Garden.

God made a special promise to Adam and Eve that, one day, He would send One who would remove sin and have victory over Satan (Read Genesis 3: 1 – 15).

Learning from the story of Creation

The story of creation teaches us three important lessons in our Christian life.

1. God is the Creator of man

"God made man from the dust of the earth." The first thing that we learn from this story is that God has the power to create the world and all that is in it. The serpent, which is the form Satan took, is God's enemy. He was planning to spoil God's beautiful creation by trying to get Adam and Eve to obey him instead of God.

2. How sin entered the world

Adam and Eve disobeyed and sinned against God. Through them, all humanity sinned. That is why we call Adam and Eve's sin, *"the original sin."* Since then, every person born has a sinful nature that does not want to please God. St. Paul explains this in his letter to the Romans, saying: "*Therefore, just as sin entered the world through one man (Adam) and death through sin (separation from God) and in this way death came to all men.*" (Romans 5: 12). Also in the next verses St. Paul says: "*Death reigned from the time of Adam to the time of Moses, even over those who did not sin by breaking a command, as did Adam, who was a pattern of the One to come*" (Verse 14).

You and I sin because we were born into sin. The bible teaches us that humans sin is not a series of errors, wrong actions, or bad habits. *Sin is what we are, not what we do.*

The sinful thoughts, desires, words and actions that we commit are the symptoms of the disease, not the disease itself. Therefore our sinful nature begins with our birth before we have ever done anything. Psalm 51:5 says, "Surely I have been sinner from birth, sinful from the time my mother conceived me." By nature everyone of us was born spiritually blind, spiritually dead and an enemy of God (turn to chapter one of the books).

3. How God responds to Sin

1. God told Adam and Eve that the day you they were to eat the forbidden fruit "you will surely die" (Genesis 2:17). This does not mean only physical, or, sudden death, but it means remaining in the state of death. This includes spiritual, temporal and eternal death. The tragic consequence of death is described in Genesis 3: 14-19.

"The wages of sins is death" (Romans 6: 23). This is what the Bible teaches us, and indeed man remains in the state of death. No one could pay the wages or the penalty of sin. The decree that God issued could not be contradicted.

2. God, who is love and mercy, continues to pursue mankind "Then the man and his wife heard the sounds of the Lord God as he was walking in the garden in the cool of the day... but the Lord God called the man, where are you?" (Genesis 3:8-9). God will never abandon you to the death, but He always pursue you and asks you, where are you?

3. God made the first promise of the Savior. The Lord announces that He will act to undo the damage that had been done, *"and I will put enmity between you and the woman and between YOUR OFFSPRING and HER. He will crush your head and you will strike His heel"* (Genesis 3: 15).

According to the prophecies, "the woman's offspring" is our Lord Jesus Christ and "the serpent" is Satan. Therefore, when God promised, "the woman's offspring will crush the head of the serpent," it meant our Lord Jesus Christ would later overcome Satan and sin.

Our Lord Jesus Christ came down from heaven, was born of the Virgin Mary, fulfilled God's law, and died on the Cross for the sins of the whole world. He paid the wages of the sin, and fulfilled God's decree. He died for your sins and mine. He did not do this for Himself because He was perfect. He was willing to take the punishment for our sins because He loved us. So He died on the Cross, was buried and rose again after three days.

Discuss with your Friends

- Reading the story of creation we learned three important facts, discuss them with your leader and friends. What are the applications of these three facts on your personal life?
- Go back and read Genesis 3: 1-19; read it in your group and find signs of spiritual and moral death; underline words like, "death," "curse," "fear," "enmity," do you see these in your life, in your friends, or even in your school? how can we overcome these signs?
- Jesus Christ was punished instead of us. How do you feel towards Jesus Christ? Discuss that with your friends.

From The book of Common Prayer

At the third hour and at all times, we worship the living Cross,
we sign ourselves with it on our foreheads;
it is our hope and our reliance,
it delivers us from the evil one,
and his power day and night.
At the third hour,
Adam ate the fruit of death in Eden, from the tree,
and at the sixth hour, the Lord of the world ascended the Cross,
for the sake of His servant who had sinned.
At the ninth hour,
He wrote the deed of his deliverance,
on the Cross and restored him to Eden, his inheritance.

2. Abraham, Isaac, and Jacob, Our Fathers in Faith

The promise of a savior, that God made to Adam and Eve, continued through many centuries. God had to prepare humans for the fulfillment of His promise. He did this gradually by calling men who heard His voice and obeyed Him.

A man called Abraham was living with his tribe, his father and his family. One day, God invited Abraham to believe in Him and gave him a mission. Abraham had to leave his country and go to an unknown place.

God promised him that he would produce a great nation, but Abraham had no children. (Read, Genesis 12: 1 – 6 "The call of Abraham" & Geneses 15: 1 – 6 "God's covenant with Abraham"). God fulfilled His promise to Abraham and Sarah by giving them a son named Isaac. His wife Sarah, in her old age, gave birth to Isaac who would continue the covenant that God made with his father Abraham. (Genesis, 18: 1 – 15 & 21: 1 – 8).

Jacob

Jacob is the grandson of Abraham his father was Isaac Abraham's son. The Bible tells us that Jacob was the father of twelve sons who became the leaders of the twelve tribes of Israel. Jacob, like his ancestors participated in the covenant with God that promised a great land and many descendants. He is portrayed as a very human character with a wide range of emotions and actions, both good and bad. Jacob is a repentant brother, and a kind father, but he is also a trickster who steals his brother Esau's birthright and his father's blessing (Read, Genesis 25: 29 – 34 & 27: 1 – 29). It is no wonder that Jacob's name means "supplanter" or "heel grabber."

In a dream, God renews the covenant promised to Jacob, and in another dream, God changes Jacob's name to Israel. Jacob's descendants thus became known as the Israelites. His story reveals that God's blessing continues to work even through flawed human beings.

And the promise of the savior continues...

What Do we learn from the story of the Patriarchs?

- Abraham, Isaac, and Jacob were called *patriarchs*, which means, *old fathers*, because they were our ancestors in faith. From their descendant's Jesus Christ was born.

- God gave promises to the patriarchs that were then fulfilled in the person of Jesus Christ. St. Paul says, in his letter to Galatians, "If you belong to Christ, then you are Abraham's seed and heirs according to the promise" (Galatians, 3: 29).

  Each one of us is a part of these ancient promises. Like the many faithful people who have gone before us, we too are the descendants of Abraham and Sarah, believers in the One God, and members of God's family. We too are heirs to a special, intimate relationship with the Holy One.

- As God spoke to Abraham, He is still speaking to us through His Son Jesus Christ. The Word of God for us is the life, death, and resurrection of Jesus Christ. The Word of God calls us to get out of our selfishness, and to live in fellowship with Him and with others.

- Abraham had the courage to move his family miles and miles away from home. He loved God, and God loved him. Abraham knew God only wanted the best for him. Likewise, God wants the best for everyone of us. When we have faith in Him, we can be brave enough to do anything.

- Our life is full of promises, projects, and aspirations, just like the life of the patriarchs. If we know how to understand these promises, we will discover that these are God's promises to everyone of us. God is calling us to trust Him and to be His friends, as He called Abraham His friend. God will fulfill His promises if you trust Him and have faith in Him.

Discuss with your Friends

- ➢ What is the Word of God for you?
- ➢ God is calling us to be His friends. Have you felt this call in your life? Write a story about that feeling.

- Make a time line showing important changes in your life. When you finish, think about how God was with you through each change.
- Write a prayer in which you express your thanks to God for guiding you through life.

Joseph, Son of Jacob

The promise of God continue through the stories and the persons of the Old Testament. In the book of Genesis we read about the story of Joseph. He was Jacob's favorite son because he was the son of Rachel, Jacob's favorite wife. His brothers' jealousy was further fueled by Joseph's reports to his father of their wrongdoing. Also, the giving of the special coat implied that Joseph would receive the blessing, which is usually reserved for the firstborn.

Joseph had two dreams, which revealed that he would have a place of authority. Joseph freely told this to his brothers, and they hated him all the more (read Genesis 37: 5 – 10).

One day Joseph's ten brothers took their flocks of sheep to graze at Shechem. Joseph's father sent him to see how his brothers and their flocks were doing. When the brothers saw Joseph approaching them, they planned to kill him. The brothers' sinful jealousy was now leading them to do a terrible thing. That is how sin develops. It often begins with just a thought and then becomes an action.

Reuben urged his brothers not to kill Joseph. So instead, they threw Joseph into an empty water hole. Judah persuaded the brothers to sell Joseph. He was sold and taken to Egypt.

Joseph spent many years in Egypt working as slave and then he was falsely accused and put in jail; But God was working all these painful experiences for the benefit of Joseph and for the fulfillment of His promise. Remember that God works all things for the good of those who love Him (Romans 8: 28)

When Pharaoh had a dream and nobody could interpret it (read Genesis 41: 1 –7), his servants recommended

Joseph to interpret the dream (read Genesis 41: 25 – 43). When Pharaoh saw the wisdom of Joseph, he decided to appoint him governor of Egypt.

The years of famine came, as God revealed to Pharaoh in his dreams. Joseph's brothers needed food so they went to Egypt to buy grain. There Joseph met his brothers and reconciled with them. Joseph invited his father Jacob and his eleven brothers to come and live in Egypt, bringing all their families with them.

Lessons learned from the story of Joseph

Joseph's story encourages us to forgive others, even when we have been unjustly treated by them. Whenever we have been greatly wronged, remembering Joseph will offer us hope and courage.

In our Christian life we learn from Joseph's story *three important* things: 1. We are part of God's plan; 2. We have to struggle against the sin in our life; and 3. Forgiveness.

1. We are part of God's plan

Read Genesis 50: 15–21

After Joseph's tearful reconciliation with his brothers, he tells them that their past treatment of him enabled him to save them from the famine. Because he ended up in Egypt and rose to power, he could now invite them to stay as guests of the Pharaoh.

Joseph realized that good came out of an evil act. He saw the events of his family's life as part of God's plan to preserve life and to make sure that the covenant continued.

Joseph's insight does not justify what his brothers did, but it does help us realize that good can come out of tragic events. It is often hard for us to understand why something bad is happening. But, as time passes, we often gain perspective and insight. These are the rewards of trust and faith.

2. Struggling against sin

Read Genesis 39: 7–18

Potiphar's wife wanted to make love with Joseph, but Joseph refused this great wickedness and sin against God. God tells us that making love like this is only for a man and woman who are married. What she asked him to do was wrong. We must, like Joseph, decide what to do when someone asks us to do something wrong. Whatever age we are, 14 or 90, we are struggling with sin. The key word is "struggle".

When we commit sin we do not sin against man but against God; that is why Joseph told Potiphar's wife, "How then could I do such a wicked thing and sin against God?" (Genesis 39: 9). The Bible symbolizes our spiritual life, and how to equip ourselves against sin much like how a soldier puts his armor on, and prepare himself, for battle;

> *"Finally, be strong in the Lord and in his mighty*
> *power. [11] Put on the full armor of God, so that you*
> *can take your stand against the devil's schemes. [12]*
> *For our struggle is not against flesh and blood, but*
> *against the rulers, against the authorities, against*
> *the powers of this dark world and against the spiritual*
> *forces of evil in the heavenly realms. [13] Therefore*
> *put on the full armor of God, so that when the day of*
> *evil comes, you may be able to stand your ground,*
> *and after you have done everything, to stand. [14]*
> *Stand firm then, with the belt of truth buckled around*
> *your waist, with the breastplate of righteousness in*
> *place, [15] and with your feet fitted with the readiness*
> *that comes from the gospel of peace. [16] In addition*
> *to all this, take up the shield of faith, with which*
> *you can extinguish all the flaming arrows of the evil*
> *one. [17] Take the helmet of salvation and the sword*
> *of the Spirit, which is the word of God"* (Ephesians
> 6: 10-17).

Our resistance in the fight against sin does not come

from our own strength, but it comes from the Holy Spirit; it comes when, by faith, we put on the spiritual armor of the Lord. The bible teaches us when temptation attacks us we must kill it by the Spirit (Romans 8: 13). Out of all the armor God gives us to fight Satan, only one piece is used for "killing," the *sword*. It is called the sword of the spirit (Ephesians 6: 17). So when the bible instructs us to kill sin by the spirit, this mean "to depend on the spirit, especially his sword." The sword of the spirit is God's word and his promises for us.

When faith has the first place in my heart I am satisfied with Christ and His promises. This is what Jesus meant when He said, "*I am the bread of life. Whoever comes to me will never go hungry, and whoever believes in me will never be thirsty*" (John 6: 35). When my hunger and thirst for joy, meaning and passion are satisfied by the presence and promises of Christ, the power of sin is broken.

3. Forgiveness

We saw in Joseph's story how his brothers felt when they hurt him and they apologized to him. We learned also how Joseph forgave their mistakes, and explained to them that it was God's plan for him to come to Egypt. Apologizing is not only saying, "I'm sorry", but also living the "sorry", we said. In order to live forgiveness and experience it we have to:

- *Face it*. You have to face the fact that you really made a mistake, that it is your fault, and that you sinned. Do not blame anyone else. Take full responsibility for your actions.
- *Feel it*. Stop and think about how you hurt the other person. Think about how you hurt God. Take a little time to feel the sadness you ought to feel before you actually say you are sorry.
- *Fix it*. A real apology is not just a matter of words, but actions as well. Truly sorry people make amends. They pay for what was stolen,

replace what was broken, or try to repair the damage done to someone's reputation.

- *Forsake it.* It is not enough to confess, we must repent. To repent means to turn away from our sins and go in a different direction.

Discuss with your Friends

- Reading Joseph's story, we realize that we are part of God's plan. Do you feel your own life, as a student, or your family's life is a part of God's plan? Share with your friends a story in which you realize that your life is a part of God's plan.
- You have just had a fight with your friend, and you hurt him. After a while, you feel sorry about it. What would you do in order to experience forgiveness from your friend? We talked briefly about the practical steps to take, discuss this advice in your group with your leader.

Saint Jacob of Sarug Supplication

O Father, Son, and Holy Spirit,
guard me in my youth, I have knocked at Your door in faith.
Answer me in Your compassion.

Unveil my eyes that I may behold Your mercy and praise Your name.
Have mercy upon me,
for I have taken refuge in Your loving-kindness.

Grant me, our Lord, as I have asked of You, a pure heart,
and instill in my mind the wisdom of life from out of Your fullness.
May the arm of the Spirit help me against the evil one.

Seal me with Your name,
and save my life from destruction.
I have loved Your name, O Lord,
and have followed after You,
put me not to shame,
rather let Your right hand cover me, as You always do.

All my will is only this,
that I belong to You and serve You,
O gracious and merciful Lord.
From You I have received mercy and compassion; do not disappoint me.

This supplication is said at Sunday evening prayers during the time of Holy Lent.

3. The Liberation from Egypt

We have seen how Jacob's sons were invited to be guests in Egypt. However, their descendents stayed in the land of Egypt lasted for a few centuries. Pharaoh began to worry when Jacob's descendents became numerous so he forced them to become hard laborers and ordered them to build his cities (Read, Exodus, 1: 8–14).

The Hebrew people started to pray to God for their salvation from the hand of Pharaoh. They asked God to remember the promises He made to their ancestors, Abraham, Isaac and Jacob. God answered the prayers of His suffering people by choosing a man named *Moses* to liberate them from slavery, and to lead them to the land God had promised to their fathers. (Read, Exodus 3: 1–12)

When Pharaoh refused to let the Israelites go, God sent *ten plagues* to convince Pharaoh to cooperate. After the tenth plague, Pharaoh gave the Hebrews permission to leave Egypt. God opened the Red Sea to let them cross it. This crossing was the symbol of liberation from "slavery" to "freedom" (Read, Exodus 14: 5–25).

All these stories are found in the second book of the Bible called, *Exodus,* which means, "exit", "departure", or "going out". It is given this name because it tells us about the "departure" or "the exit" of the Jewish people from Egypt.

Learning from the story of the Exodus

What happens in the Old Testament has many symbolic meanings in the New Testament and in the life of Jesus Christ. The stories of the Exodus has many spiritual and practical meanings in our Christian life.

1. We are the new people of God

Christians believe that Jesus Christ is "the New Moses" who liberated us from the "slavery of sin", and He established with us a "new and eternal alliance." Therefore, Christians are "the New People of God" who have been saved from the "Spiritual Pharaoh", which is Satan.

In the New Testament in St. Peter's first letter we read, "You are the chosen people...A people belonging to God, that you may declare the praises of Him who called you out of darkness into His wonderful light" (1 Peter 2: 9). We are going to study more about this point in the fourth station, *the holy church*.

According to the teaching of Church Fathers, especially St. Ephraim (303-373 A.D.) Christian baptism is a "re-entry into Paradise." Biblical and symbolic expressions like, "new creation," "born again," into the "spiritual womb" of the baptismal water, remind us of the spiritual state of Adam in Paradise before the fall. St. Ephraim compares the "Promised Land" to "Paradise." In Christian baptism he suggests that the baptized crosses the "Red Sea" and the "Jordan River" like the Israelites did thousands of years ago. In addition, the escape from bondage in Egypt evokes similarly the escape of a Christian in baptism from "the domain of Satan and death." Subsequently, through Christian baptism we are re-admitted into Paradise.

The newly born Christian, after baptism, puts on the "robe of glory" and the "robe of praise" with which Adam and Eve were clothed before falling into sin. St. Jacob of Sarugh (451-521 A.D.) says, "The robe of glory, that was stolen (by Satan) among the trees of Paradise, I put on in the water of baptism." St. Ephraim stresses this topic, "Instead of fig leaves God clothed man with glory in the baptismal water."

2. We are being set free in Jesus Christ

We learned in the first chapter how death entered the world; mankind remained under the authority of death and Satan until God fulfilled his promise by sending a savior. When Jesus came down from heaven, died and was resurrected, He vanquished sin and Satan, setting us free from the power and authority of the sinful nature we inherited from Adam and Eve.

When we believe in Jesus Christ and we are baptized,

we receive Him. God gives us the gift of the New Life. As God, by His power, open the Red Sea and drowned Pharaoh and his soldiers, likewise, when we believe and receive the gift of Baptism, God, by His grace and power, drowns the old nature and its power and empowers us with the gifts of the New Life in Christ. This is what the New Testament teaches us;

> *Don't you know that all of us who were baptized into Christ Jesus were baptized into his death? [4] We were therefore buried with him through baptism into death in order that, just as Christ was raised from the dead through the glory of the Father, we too may live a new life. [5] For if we have been united with him in a death like his, we will certainly also be united with him in a resurrection like his. [6] For we know that our old self was crucified with him so that the body ruled by sin might be done away with, that we should no longer be slaves to sin— [7] because anyone who has died has been set free from sin* (Romans 6: 3-7).

Through Jesus Christ, we are set free from Satan, death and sin. This is the true freedom; it is a gift that has been given to us by God Almighty.

What does freedom mean for us as young Christians? How do we practice Christian freedom? Before answering this question, I invite you to look at the successful spiritual life of a young man named Ken Clark.

A big part of Ken's spiritual success is the fact that he begins each day by expressing both his dependence on God and his desire to walk closely with Him. Ken's prayer begins like this, "Your Word is so true. You are the Good Shepherd. O Lord, keep me from wondering away from You today. Help me to realize that You will keep me safe and provide everything I need if I will just stay close to You. Thank you for loving me in Christ my Lord. Amen."

In the New Testament, Jesus compares Himself to

the Good Shepherd and His followers to sheep. Sheep are dependent animals. As long as they remain close to their owners, they enjoy prosperity, protection, and peace. However, as soon as they wonder away from their keeper, they open themselves to danger and possible death.

Freedom does not mean, "not to obey," or "do whatever I like to do." Liberty is to be guided by the law of God and by His truth. Jesus said, "If you hold My teachings you are My disciples, then you will know the truth and ***the truth will set you free***. I tell you the truth, everyone who sins is a slave to sin. Now a slave has no permanent place in the family but a son belongs to it forever. So if the Son (Who is Jesus Christ) sets you free, you will be free indeed" (John 8: 31-32, 34-36).

Ken's success was because the Spirit of God guided him. He enjoyed his liberty in walking with God and letting Him lead his life. He kept these verses from the Psalms in mind when he was talking with God,

"The Lord is my shepherd, I shall not be in want. He makes me lie down in green pastures, He restores my soul. He guides me in paths of righteousness for His name's sake" (Psalm 23: 1 – 3). "Come, let us bow down in worship, let us kneel before the Lord our Maker for He is our God and we are the people of His pasture, the flock under His care" (Psalm 95: 6 - 7).

As we read the Gospel, we understand that we can enjoy our own liberty by following and practicing the teachings of our Lord Jesus Christ. We enjoy liberty when we recognize our good qualities; When we discover the gifts of the New Life that is available to everyone who believe and confesses Jesus as his Lord and Savior, when we are available to reach out to others and tell them about Christ who lives in us and reign in our hearts and minds and when we learn how to use new discoveries made by the community. We enjoy liberty when we decide to be and to do the best for our family, community, and country. This is the promise of Jesus, "let your light shine before others, that they may see your good deeds and glorify your Father in heaven" (Matthew 5: 16).

3. Nothing that happens is ever out of God's plan

Read Exodus 14: 5 - 29

When we read the story of the exodus from Egypt, we see how the Jewish people panicked and rebelled against God and Moses as they saw the approaching armies of Egypt. They said to Moses, "Was it because there were no graves in Egypt that you have taken us away to die in the wilderness?" (Exodus14: 11). In their complaining, they were forgetting something very important about God, namely that *nothing that happens is ever out of God's control.* Sometimes it seems as if things are out of control. Natural disasters like earthquakes or hurricanes destroy whole cities. People you love may be injured in an accident or die of a terrible disease. Perhaps your family is having a hard time. These difficult situations are hard to understand, but the Bible teaches us that God is sovereign. He is the ruler over all things, and He works things out according to His own plan. Nothing happens unless God in His wisdom allows it. We can't always understand why things happen, but we do know that God is in control.

When things got very bad, God showed the people in a most amazing way that He is the ruler over all. "Moses stretched his hand, as God had instructed. And the sea divided making a path of escape" (Exodus14: 21). Even the waves of the sea are under His command. He controls everything that touches your life and He will allow only what is best for you.

You may not understand why some things happen or how they will work out, but you can have faith and believe that God is working out His plan. When things seem out of control and you are tempted to panic, don't! Instead, thank God that He is in control and ask Him to help you trust and wait patiently for Him to work things out in His own way.

Discuss with your Friends

- In our discussion we talked about liberty saying that, "*liberty is to be guided by the law of God, and His truth… we gain our liberty by following and practicing the teachings of our Lord Jesus Christ."* How difficult is it to practice Christian liberty at your school, in your home and with your family? What are the difficulties that you face in practicing Christian liberty?

- In this discussion, we learned that, *"nothing that happens is ever out of God's control"*. Do you feel that your life in school, family, and with friends is under God's control? Tell us a story in which you really realized that God is protecting your life. If you don't feel that your life is under God's control, how can you place it under His control? Tell us how you can help some of your friends to be lead by the Spirit of God.
- Freedom is a gift that you receive when you put your trust in Christ and His promise, do you want to have this freedom? Jesus said, "ask and you shall receive" (Matthew 7:7, Luke 11:9) Ask Jesus in your personal prayer to empower you with His freedom, talk to your leader and pastor about your desire to have the power and the freedom that Christ give to everyone who ask Him in faith.

The Sacrificial Lamb

In the Book of Exodus we read an amazing story of how God instructed the people to buy a lamb, kill it and eat it in a very specific way.

> *The LORD said to Moses and Aaron in Egypt, 2 “This month is to be for you the first month, the first month of your year. 3 Tell the whole community of Israel that on the tenth day of this month each man is to take a lamb for his family, one for each household. 4 If any household is too small for a whole lamb, they must share one with their nearest neighbor, having taken into account the number of people there are. You are to determine the amount of lamb needed in accordance with what each person will eat. 5 The animals you choose must be year-old males without defect, and you may take them from the sheep or the goats. 6 Take care of them until the fourteenth day of the month, when all the members of the community of Israel must slaughter them at twilight. 7 Then they are to take some of the blood and put it on the sides and tops of the doorframes of the houses where they eat the lambs. 8 That same night they are to eat the meat roasted over the fire, along with bitter herbs, and bread made without yeast. 9 Do not eat the meat raw or boiled in water, but roast it over a fire—with the head, legs and internal organs. 10 Do not leave any of it till morning; if some is left till morning, you must burn it. 11 This is how you are to eat it: with your cloak tucked into your belt, your sandals on your feet and your staff in your hand. Eat it in haste; it is the LORD’s Passover...*
>
> *“Pick out and take lambs for yourselves*

according to your families, and kill the Passover lamb. [22] And you shall take a bunch of hyssop, dip it in the blood that is in the basin, and strike the lintel and the two doorposts with the blood that is in the basin. And none of you shall go out of the door of his house until morning. [23] For the LORD will pass through to strike the Egyptians; and when He sees the blood on the lintel and on the two doorposts, the LORD will pass over the door and not allow the destroyer to come into your houses to strike you. [24] And you shall observe this thing as an ordinance for you and your sons forever. [25] It will come to pass when you come to the land which the LORD will give you, just as He promised, that you shall keep this service. [26] And it shall be, when your children say to you, 'What do you mean by this service?' [27] that you shall say, 'It is the Passover sacrifice of the LORD, who passed over the houses of the children of Israel in Egypt when He struck the Egyptians and delivered our households'" (Exodus 12: 1-11, 21-27).

The only way for the people of the Old Testament to be delivered from slavery was to trust, believe and obey what the Lord commanded them to do. The blood of a sacrificial Lamb was the only sign of their salvation from bondage.

After the Exodus from slavery to freedom, the Lord commanded the people to continue to sacrifice a Lamb every year to remember how the Lord delivered them from slavery. However, all these lambs were not able to uproot the sin and its consequences from the life of man.

Thousands of years passed, and we hear John the Baptist in the New Testament telling us that Jesus is the Lamb of God who takes away the sin of the world (John 1: 29, 36). John the Baptist is reminding us of the Lamb in the Old Testament.

From these two passages in the Old and New Testament we understand that everything that the Lord commanded the People of the Old Testament to do was a symbol that will later be fullfiled in the the life of Christ. Jesus was called a "Lamb who takes away the sin of the world" because He was crucified and shed His blood on the Cross.

You and I are saved from the bondage of sin when we believe. As it was in the Old Testament, it is the same for Christians. The only way for us to be saved is to believe and trust in what was done on the Cross. Baptism is our participation in the life, death, and resurrection of our Lord Jesus Christ (Roman 6:3-7). The differences between the Lamb of the Old Testament and the Lamb of the New Testament is that in the Old Testament people were repeating it for many years. Jesus in the New Testament was sacrificed once and for all. There is no need for us to sacrifice Lambs anymore, because Jesus is the eternal sacrifice. Our part is to receive, believe, trust and confess. The New Testament explains these connections;

> [18] *knowing that you were not redeemed with corruptible things, like silver or gold, from your aimless conduct received by tradition from your fathers,* [19] *but with the precious* ***blood of Christ****, as of* ***a lamb without blemish and without spot****.* [20] *He indeed was foreordained before the foundation of the world, but was manifest in these last times for your sake.* [21] *Through Him you believe in God, who raised Him from the dead and gave Him glory, so that your faith and hope are in God* (1 Peter 1: 18-21).

> *For indeed Christ,* ***our Passover****, was sacrificed for us* (1corinthian 5:7).

> [11] *But Christ came as High Priest of the good things to come, with the greater and more perfect tabernacle not made with hands, that is, not of this creation.*
> [12] *Not with the blood of goats and calves, but with* ***His own blood*** *He entered the Most Holy Place once for all, having obtained eternal redemption.*
> [13] *For if the blood of bulls and goats and the ashes*

of a heifer, sprinkling the unclean, sanctifies for the purifying of the flesh,
[14] *how much more shall the blood of Christ, who through the eternal Spirit offered Himself without spot to God, cleanse your conscience from dead works to serve the living God?*
[15] *And for this reason He is the Mediator of the new covenant, by means of death, for the redemption of the transgressions under the first covenant, that those who are called may receive the promise of the eternal inheritance* (Hebrews 9: 11-15).

From the Common Book of prayer

Moses with his staff,
divided the sea before the host and Israel crossed over.
Our Lord Jesus,
by the Cross of the light,
opened Sheol (hell) and raised the dead.

Blessed is Christ,
Who trod for us the way of life,
from the grave to Paradise.
The Cross is light,
and clothes its worshipers in the light,
and in the garment of glory.

From the depths to the heights,
it lifts up him who looks upon it,
and takes refuge in it at all times.
By it, Lord,
give peace to those above and below,
and keep Your Church and her children.

4. The People of the Old Testament wait for a New Hope

The people of the Old Testament entered the Promised Land and became a nation. They remembered how God was faithful to the promises He made to their ancestors Abraham, Isaac and Jacob how He liberated them from the slavery of Egypt, how He opened the Red Sea for them; and how He protected them in the desert. God made a covenant with the patriarchs and the people of the Old Testament. The people could not be faithful to the covenant. They continued to sin against God. They abandoned Him, surrounding themselves with immorality and idolatry.

God sent men called *prophets* to rebuke the people and to show them how grave their sins were. The prophets also announced a message of hope that the Messiah, who is our Lord Jesus Christ, would come as Savior to bear the Cross, wear a crown, and save us from sin.

God allowed His people to feel the hopelessness of trying to save themselves through the Law, or the written covenant, but He never allowed them to fall into despair. Throughout the Old Testament times, He continually gave them signs and prophecies about the coming of the Messiah, Who would deliver them from their terrible predicament.

As we learned earlier, the promises and the covenant that God made with Adam and Eve, Abraham, Isaac and Jacob would be fulfilled in the person of Jesus Christ. He is the Messiah, whom all the prophets talked about. He is the fulfillment of all the prophecies and all the promises to the people of the Old Testament.

Moses said: "The Lord your God will raise up for you a prophet like me from among your own brothers. You must listen to Him" (Deuteronomy 18: 15).

Isaiah, who served as a prophet from 740 B.C. to 681 B. C., foretells the birth, suffering, and death of Jesus Christ. He said: "Therefore the Lord Himself will give a sign: the virgin will bear a child and will give birth to a son and will call Him Emmanuel which means "God is with us" (Isaiah 7: 14). The virgin implies the Virgin Mary mother of God, and the Son, which will be called Emmanuel, our Lord Jesus Christ.

Isaiah also predicted our Lord's suffering and death saying:

> *He was despised and rejected by men, a man of sorrow, and familiar with suffering. Like one from whom men hide their faces, He was despised, and we esteemed Him not. Surely He took up our infirmities and carried our sorrows [...] He was crushed for our iniquities; the punishment that brought us peace was upon Him, and by His wounds we are healed* (Isaiah 53: 3 – 6).

Covenant is a powerful word in the Bible, with deep religious significance, because it expresses the intimate relationship between God and God's people. At its most basic level, a covenant is a promise between both parties involved to do certain things.

The Bible tells us that the covenant is always God's initiative. He wants to lead His people to a better way of life. However, the people must respond to God's offer as a sign of their faith in Him.

Throughout the history of salvation God established three types of Covenants:

1. The Oral Covenant was with Abraham when God promised him that his seed would be God's people if they obeyed Him. The sign of this covenant was circumcision. Its purpose was to demonstrate the necessity for God's people to be different, set apart from the rest of the world, and to establish a nation and a family. From that nation salvation (Jesus Christ) would come.

2. The Written Covenant. God established the "Law" through Moses. The purpose of the Law was to define sin by outlining perfection, that which was required to return to the presence of God. This experience would show man that he could never earn salvation on his own. Adam and Eve had one commandment to keep; now there were ten. In addition, there were 613 laws that had to be kept precisely. To break one was to break them all. Each transgression had to be followed by a related offering or sacrifice that established the fact that sin required atonement.

Man was caught in a never ending cycle. He would inevitably break a law, bring the required offering, and go out and break another. This futile cycle continued until Jesus Christ offered Himself as the last living sacrifice on behalf of mankind.

3. The Blood Covenant. God has established this as the fulfillment of the oral and written covenants before it. In keeping with its provisions, all who believe that Jesus Christ is the Son of God and accept and confess that He is their Lord and Savior, the Messiah who provided the way to the Kingdom, will receive the gift of salvation, not by their own efforts but by the virtue of being a part of Christ through baptism and a life of faith, thus enabled to share His inheritance.

Lessons learned from this station

In this second station of our journey, we learned what God's plan was for the people of the Old Testament. This plan was to prepare them for the coming of Messiah, Who is our Lord Jesus Christ.

- We saw how God created man and put him in the garden, but man sinned against God. Adam and Eve were punished, and through them all humanity. However, God promised them that He would send One who would save man and destroy Satan and sin.
- God's promises continued with our Old Fathers in the faith, Abraham, Isaac, Jacob, and Joseph.
- We learned how God, by His powerful hand, liberated the people of the Old Testament from the hand of Pharaoh. Christians are the "new people of God." Jesus Christ is the "New Moses" Who liberated us from sin.
- The people continued to sin. God sent men called "prophets" to remind the people of the promises given to them, and to announce the new hope to the people.
- Why do we read the stories of the Old Testament?

The Old Testament was the Bible used by Christ and the apostles. Almost uniformly, the word "scripture" or "scriptures" in the New Testament refer to the Old Testament. For about two decades after Christ the only parts of the New Testament were fragmentary accounts of the life and teachings of Jesus Christ. During this period when a vital Church was extending its influence into Syria, Asia Minor, and North Africa, the basis for preaching and teaching was the Old Testament as reinterpreted by Jesus and His early followers.

The Old Testament belongs not to the Jewish people alone but to all. It is the account of the ways in which God worked. It is the summary of what He has demanded, the record of His preparation for Christ's coming, the best work of art in which to envision the picture of His interaction with the human family through the centuries. In short, it is the indispensable foundation on which the New Testament is built.

To understand the Old Testament as Christian Scriptures one must see it through the eyes of Jesus and His disciples, and that is exactly what we tried to do in this station. And that is what the Lord did with the two disciples of Emmaus. He taught them from Moses and the prophets of the Old Testament concerning Himself.

The stories of the Old Testament were especially inspired by God's Spirit to grasp the meaning of God's revelatory words and deeds and the direction in which they were moving. In all these stories, we saw ourselves as part of God's plan. He always invites us to be His friend, to build a new story, a new land for us and for Him. He liberated us from sin, and He invites us to help Him to liberate people from their sins. We have the task to show to the world the light of our Lord Jesus Christ.

We are invited to leave our "old life" in sin and follow His steps, as Abraham, Isaac, and Jacob were invited to follow God's call, and to leave their old lives.

Remember! You also learned in the first station that since you were born God has given you a mission to fulfill, a purpose to follow in your life. You have to choose your goals and share your Christian experience with the world. That is what our Lord Jesus Christ commanded us before He was lifted up into heaven,

"Go into all the world and preach the good news to all

creation. Whoever believes and is baptized will be saved, but whoever does not believe will be condemned" (Mark 16: 15 – 16).

Saint Ephraim Petition

Grant me o my Lord, while I keep watch,
to stand before Thee awake
and if I fall asleep again
let my slumber be sinless.

In my wake if I offend,
by Thy grace, I be atoned
In slumber if I shall sin
Thy mercy will me pardon.

By the Cross of Your meekness
grant me a peaceful slumber.
And save me from evil dreams,
As well from phantoms unclean.

Send me an angel of light;
That will protect all my limbs.
Save me from unholy lust;
By Thy live Body I ate.

May I rest and sleep in calm;
And Your Blood be my guardian.
Giving freedom to the soul;
Which is but Thy own image.

Third Station

MEETING JESUS OF NAZARETH

"As they talked and discussed their things with each other, Jesus Himself came up and walked along with them" (Luke 24: 15).

Who is Jesus Christ?

We have learned in the second station of our journey that the story of the people of the Old Testament is part of our story. All our fathers in faith, Abraham, Isaac, Jacob, Joseph, were looking for the fulfillment of the promise. The coming of our Lord Jesus Christ is the fulfillment of these promises.

Through the coming of our Lord Jesus Christ, God showed Himself to us; God became man; that is why we call Jesus the "Incarnated God." The letter to the Hebrews described this fact by saying: "In the past God spoke to our forefathers through the prophets at many times and in various ways, but in these days He has spoken to us by His Son" (Hebrew 1: 1).

Two thousand years ago, Jesus Christ asked His disciples, "Who do you say I am?" (Matthew 16: 16). Each one of us, every Christian generation must give an answer to this question. Jesus Christ is our God and Savior. He is our friend Who cares about us and loves us.

Attention As we did in the second station, you have to put your Bible beside this devotional book. I did not write the text for you, because I want you to go by yourself and open your Bible alongside these notes. Remember always that one of the goals of this journey is to be familiar with the Holy Scripture.

In this station, I added also *deep understandings*, which are some questions that inspire you to understand the text. In the next point, *observation,* you will read some notes that explain the text for you.

As the story of the two disciples of Emmaus continues we learn that as they were talking and discussing things Jesus Himself came up and walked along with them (turn to Luke 24: 15). However, they did not recognize Him because they were busy and worried about many things around them. In this third station of our journey we will learn about Jesus Christ who, many times, walks with us, but we don not recognize Him, because we are lost with many other things.

I invite you to say this prayer before you start the third station

In the name of the Father, the Son, and the Holy Spirit, One true God,

to Whom be glory and upon us mercy and compassion for ever and ever. Amen

Our heavenly Father

We offer You praises and thanksgivings

for the Incarnation of Your son Jesus Christ.

Thank You Lord

for redeeming us through the Blood Covenant.

Dear Lord:

As You came up and walked with the disciples of Emmaus

And showed Yourself to them

That they may learn about You;

I invite You dear Lord

To come and walk with me

Teach me Lord about You;

Open my eyes to recognize You

And confess You as my Lord and my Savior. Amen

1. Jesus is God

Scripture readings: John 14: 5–11 & 20: 24 –29

1. Go through John 14: 5–11 again. List all the claims Jesus made about being equal with God. What is the most convincing to you?
2. How did Jesus react to Thomas in John 20: 26–29? What does Jesus' reaction tell you about Him?

Observation

The first thing we should learn about Jesus Christ is that He is God. In these two readings, we saw Jesus announce Himself as God, "I am the way and the truth and the life. No one comes to the Father except through Me. If you really knew Me, you would know My Father as well. From now on, you do know Him and have seen Him" (John 14: 6–7).

However, some of His disciples, like Thomas, did not understand what Jesus was saying. Thomas was an honest follower though always the skeptic, so he asked, "Lord, we do not know where You are going, so how can we know the way?"

Also, in the second reading, we saw Thomas asking for evidence to believe that Jesus had risen from the dead. Jesus showed Himself and asked Thomas to reach out his hand and put it in Jesus' side. Then Thomas believed and announced Him as "his Lord and his God".

Many people, like Thomas, become frustrated because they cannot understand how Jesus could be both human and divine; two distinctively different natures at the same time. If you want to understand this difficult truth, look at a frozen glass of water. What does ice consist of? Is it frozen water or water? Take another glass of water and ask what element does water consist of? It is water. Ice and water are two manifestations of the same element. Ice and water have different properties, but they come from the same source. It is the same with the humanity and the divinity of Jesus; they are different manifestations, but they come from the same source. Even when we have doubts and questions, the fact remains that JESUS IS GOD.

Jesus did not scold Thomas because he did not believe. Jesus wanted Thomas to believe so He encouraged him to "reach out and touch Him." When we are having a bad day, when everything seems to be going wrong, when we are sad, we too can have a hard time believing that Jesus is with us. Jesus knows it will not help to scold us for not believing. Instead, Jesus says to us, "Come near, reach out, touch Me, I am here."

We will always have hard times believing, and will always face many questions in our lives. Nevertheless, we have to come to the Father and ask Him to help sustain and secure our faith. We have only to come to the Father in daily prayer and say, "You are our God, and Savior. Help sustain and secure us."

Application

- Write a letter to God in which you express your faith as well as your questions. Be honest with God about the doubts and questions you might have. Ask God to show you specific evidences that would help you to respond as Thomas eventually did, "My Lord and my God."

2. Jesus is our Savior

Scripture readings Luke 2: 8 – 11

1. What was the good news the angels brought to the shepherds?
2. What happened in the town of David?
3. What does Christ the Savior mean to you?

Observation

The second thing we have to learn about Jesus Christ is that *He is our Savior.* In the reading, we heard the angel proclaim "Christ the Lord as Savior." What does that mean?

We learned in the first station that Adam and Eve sinned against God. They were cast out of the garden. However, God promised them to send a Savior to take away their sins. We learned that the people of the Old Testament were waiting for a new hope, the Messiah, to save them from sin. We also learned that the Mosaic Law, or, the written covenant that the Lord gave to Moses was not able to save humanity. Man was caught in a never ending cycle

Jesus Christ came down from heaven and dwelt among us to bring us back to the Garden after being out of it for many centuries. He suffered, was crucified, and died for our sins. On the third day, He rose and took away our sins.

We were punished to die in sin before Jesus' coming. However, after the coming of Christ, we were saved by His death and resurrection. St. Paul says in his first letter to Corinthians, "For as in Adam all die, so in Christ all will be made alive" (1 Corinthians 15: 28).

What does it mean to be saved?

How are we saved? It is important for you to understand how we are saved. *Salvation is the process of sanctification, personal growth toward the image of God and, following Christ's example.* This process is made possible by grace, through our faith, and continues throughout our life. We are saved by grace through faith.

The process of salvation is a cooperative effort between man and God. It involves the past, present, and future. As Christians we say:

Past, I was saved. The letter to the Hebrews describes this by saying: "And by that will, we have been made holy through the sacrifice of the body of Jesus Christ once for all" (Hebrews 10: 10).

The term the Bible uses is "*justification,*" which means to be declared "not guilty." In scripture, justification is a verdict not a process or quality in man. God's declaration of man as innocent is just and fair because of the atoning death of Christ on the Cross where full payment for sin was exacted in blood. Therefore, the justification of the sinner is completely the work of God's grace. the man is justified not on the basis of anything he has done, but only because of what God in Christ has done for man.

> *But now the righteousness of God apart from the law is revealed, being witnessed by the Law and the Prophets,* [22] *even the righteousness of God, through faith in Jesus Christ, to all and on all who believe. For there is no difference;* [23] *for all have sinned and fall short of the glory of God,* [24] *being justified freely by His grace through the redemption that is in Christ Jesus,* [25] *whom God set forth as a propitiation by His blood, through faith, to demonstrate His righteousness, because in His forbearance God had passed over the sins that were previously committed,* [26] *to demonstrate at the present time His righteousness, that He might be just and the justifier of the one who has faith in Jesus* (Romans 3: 21-25).

Jesus made my salvation possible when He died on the Cross to redeem me from my sins. The Bible calls this *"redemption,"* which means the liberation of possession, or freeing from chains, slavery, or prison. When we say that "Jesus paid the penalty of death for our sins" We do not mean the literal sense as a price "exacted by" and "paid to" someone, but as the Savior accepting the painful consequences for the wrongful actions of others. When He took flesh, the Son of God subjected Himself to death, which came to man as a result of sin. But Christ was sinless, so death could not hold Him. It is the same way for us, death cannot hold anyone who is united with Him through the life of faith and baptism.

God's plan for salvation has been fulfilled in the person of Jesus Christ, and the way to the kingdom is through

Jesus Christ, the Son of God and the Savior of all who turn to Him. However, if, for example, I were studying the subject of math, I would not be allowed to just inform the teacher that I know the principles of that science and proceed to take a passing grade! I would be given a test. In a similar manner, professed faith is not true faith unless it has been tested in the context of life.

Present, I am being saved. I must demonstrate my faith in Christ as the Messiah in the way established by God, by trying to become as much like Him as I can through obedience. Our Lord's perfect life set the example to follow. This is a process, as St. Paul wrote, "We must all press on toward the mark of perfection" (turn to Phil 3: 12–16). This is called in the Bible, *"sanctification."* It is the step that follows justification and it refers to the spiritual growth of the believers. The process of sanctification is the work of God and the Holy Spirit through which the Christian is restored, step by step, in the image of God, righteous life, and holiness of conduct.

While justification takes place outside of man as God declares him to be righteous for Christ's sake, sanctification is divine action within man, it is the work of Christ within us. As by faith and baptism we become participants in the death and resurrection of our Lord. *Justification* is Christ action ***for me***. *Sanctification* is Christ's action ***in me***; it is the necessary result of justification. The two are inseparably connected to one another.

The Bible teaches us that the love of God was poured into our hearts by the Holy Spirit (Roman 5: 5). Good works flow out of our hearts when we are filled with the Spirit of the Lord. Good works are the evidence of faith; they never produce faith. Faith without good works is dead and good works without faith does not save. The Bible is very clear in this matter;

> *[7] Do not be deceived, God is not mocked; for whatever a man sows, that he will also reap. [8] For he who sows to his flesh will of the flesh reap corruption, but he who sows to the Spirit will of the Spirit reap everlasting life. [9] And let us not grow weary while*

doing good, for in due season we shall reap if we do not lose heart. [10] Therefore, as we have opportunity, let us do good to all, especially to those who are of the household of faith (Galatians 6: 7-10).

[14] What does it profit, my brethren, if someone
says he has faith but does not have works? Can
faith save him? [15] If a brother or sister is naked
and destitute of daily food, [16] and one of you says
to them, "Depart in peace, be warmed and filled,"
but you do not give them the things which are
needed for the body, what does it profit? [17] Thus
also faith by itself, if it does not have works, is dead.
[18] But someone will say, "You have faith, and I have
works." Show me your faith without your works, and
I will show you my faith by my works. [19] You believe
that there is one God. You do well. Even the demons
believe—and tremble! [20] But do you want to know,
O foolish man, that faith without works is dead?
[21] Was not Abraham our father justified by works
when he offered Isaac his son on the altar? [22] Do
you see that faith was working together with his
works, and by works faith was made perfect? [23] And
the Scripture was fulfilled which says, "Abraham
believed God, and it was accounted to him for
righteousness." And he was called the friend of God.
[24] You see then that a man is justified by works, and
not by faith only.[25] Likewise, was not Rahab the
harlot also justified by works when she received
the messengers and sent them out another way?
[26] For as the body without the spirit is dead, so faith
without works is dead also (James 2: 14-26).

Future, I will be saved. I must face judgment when my life, my period of testing, is over or at the Second Coming of Christ, whichever occurs first. My life will be evaluated, not by my successes or failures but by whether or not I really tried, as consequences of faith, to follow the example of perfection our Lord provided. To prove their love, Adam and Eve were expected to obey the one commandment God gave them. To prove our love for and belief in Jesus Christ as Savior, we are expected to try to follow His example in all things as our acknowledgment of His existence and acceptance of Him as Lord and Master.

For by Grace we are saved. *Grace is the supernatural assistance given to man to sanctify him for the Kingdom.* The Bible teaches us that our salvation is totally by grace; without grace, growth in Christ's image would not be possible.

At the time of judgment, grace will also compensate for the shortcomings of those whose lives showed faith. God calls us to be perfect in imitation of our Lord to prove our faith. He requires, however, only that we continually strive to do the best we can. His grace mercifully fills the void. Therefore, we continually pray; *Kiries Eleison*, Lord have mercy. Grace justifies us and sanctifies us.

> *But God, who is rich in mercy, because of His great love with which He loved us, [5] even when we were dead in trespasses, made us alive together with Christ (by grace you have been saved), [6] and raised us up together, and made us sit together in the heavenly places in Christ Jesus, [7] that in the ages to come He might show the exceeding riches of His grace in His kindness toward us in Christ Jesus. [8] For by grace you have been saved through faith, and that not of yourselves; it is the gift of God* (Ephesians 2:8-9).

> *[6] And if by grace, then it is no longer of works; otherwise grace is no longer grace. But if it is of works, it is no longer grace; otherwise work is no longer work* (Roman11: 6).

Application

- Why do we call Jesus Christ our Savior?
- In our class we said, "*salvation is the process of sanctification, personal growth toward the*

image of God and, following Christ's example." You might have been be baptized when you were a child, but this is not enough. How are you growing toward the image of God, and how are you following the example of Christ? What are the obstructions that you see around you? Discuss this, in private, with your leader, or, in public, with your friends, ask the Lord to give you strength and power to be a follower of Christ.

3. *Jesus is the best Friend we will ever have*

Scripture readings: John15:14 - 16; 1 Peter 5:7

1. Go through John 15:14 – 16. What did Jesus call his followers? What is the condition to become His friend?
2. According to St. Peter, what do we have to do to become God's friends?
3. What is friendship?

Observation

A good friend is someone we can count on, as well as being so much more.

A friend is someone with whom we can relax and just hang out, have fun and share our innermost thoughts –deep dark secrets, lofty and noble goals, or our hopes, joys and fears.

A good friend allows you a safe space to share your deepest thoughts and needs-without worry of being judged, criticized or made to feel silly for feeling the way you do.

Friends cheer each other on, laugh and cry together, and just plain commiserate and listen to each other.

That's why friends are friends.

(Bettie B. Youngs – Jennifer Leigh Youngs, *Taste Berries for Teens,* Florida, 1999, p. 52)

When Sarah moved with her family to a new community, she did not want to leave her hometown a month before her long awaited freshman year at Clark High School, but did anyone bother to consult her? No Way! Therefore, on her first day at the new school, Sarah did not know a soul. She felt ignored, stared at, forgotten, insignificant, isolated, left out, ugly, unloved, misunderstood and abandoned.

Many of us feel the same way Sarah felt in her first day at school. Many times we experience isolation, and abandonment, yet the Bible declares that we are no longer "servants" but "friends" of the Lord Jesus Christ. Jesus claimed you as His friends "I no longer call you servants... I have called you friends" (John 15: 15). Jesus is the One you can count on, relax, and share your innermost thoughts, secrets, ambitions, joys, and fears with.

Jesus cares for you, trusts you, and wants to be your friend. St. Peter urges you to "cast all your anxiety on Him because He cares for you" (1Peter 5: 7). If you really believe in Jesus Christ, listen and trust Him and He will never leave you or forsake you (Hebrew 13: 5).

How do we become friends of Jesus?

We become Jesus' friends through our *daily prayer,* when we pray alone, or with the community of believers at the Church. We share our innermost thoughts, deep dark secrets, joys, and fears with our Lord. The Lord who has chosen you to be His friend will guide you, by the power of the Holy Spirit, in the right direction. Jesus promised that the Holy Spirit will guide us to the truth; He will fill you with joy and happiness (John 16: 13).

We learn more about our friend Christ by reading the Bible and attending church. Jesus is always close to you. He knocks on the door of your heart. Open it and invite Him to enter in and be your friend.

Application

- How is Jesus compared with the friends of today?
- Do you feel that Jesus is your friend? Why or why not?
- How would your life change if you test that Jesus is the best friend you could ever have?

Supplication

Jesus, Son of the Father, be our helper,
Jesus, Son of Mary, be our protection,
Jesus, strengthen us,
Jesus, guard us,
Jesus, drive out the evil one from us,
Jesus, forgive us our offences and sins,
Jesus, have pity on us, when You judge us. Amen.

Pray with Psalms

Psalm 141

O Lord, I call to You; come quickly to me.

Hear my voice when I call You.

May my prayer be set before You like incense.

May the lifting up of my hands be like the evening sacrifice.

Set a guard over my mouth o Lord.

Keep watch over the door of my lips.

Let not my heart be drawn to what is evil,

To take part in wicked deeds with men who are evildoers.

Let me not eat of their delicacies.

4. Our Friend Jesus brings New Life

Scripture readings: John 3: 1 – 17

1. Who came to visit Jesus at night?
2. What is the condition to enter the Kingdom of God?
3. What is it that Nicodemus wanted from Jesus?

Observation

A good friend helps you become a better, wiser and more compassionate person than you might have been without that friend in your life. Friends help us grow into being who we are or someone with whom I can reveal many parts of me, even those I am meeting for the first time.

(*Taste Berries for Teens,* Florida 1999, p. 52)

In our reading, we saw one Pharisee named Nicodemus coming to Jesus to learn more about Him. Every one of us can do the same thing Nicodemus did. When we want to learn about Jesus, we have to come to Him and ask because He is our friend, Who cares about us, and loves us. We have to know more about Him and make ourselves known to Him.

Jesus showed Nicodemus the condition to enter the Kingdom of God, namely, being *"born again from the water and spirit"*. Jesus was talking about spiritual birth and about a new life that we should receive to be a Christian.

We receive new life in Christ through faith and baptism in which we are born from the water and the Spirit. Every Christian has two births; the first one is physical birth and the second one is spiritual birth. Physically we were born from the womb of our mothers, and we are born spiritually from the baptismal fount (See, John 3: 5).

When we come to church on Sunday, we are united with the rest of the church, which is the body of Christ. During Sunday's service, we submit our lives to Jesus Christ; we reveal ourselves to Him; share with Him our deepest thoughts and needs, joys and worries, and ask Him to help us grow in life and wisdom.

5. Our Friend Jesus brings Abundant Life

Scripture reading: John 10: 7 – 10

1. What did Jesus call Himself?
2. Who were the people who came before Jesus?
3. Why did Jesus come?

Observation

In this reading, Jesus compares Himself to the gate and the believers to sheep. When the sheep have to go back home, after being out all day in the pasture, if they do not go through the right gate they will be lost. Likewise, as believers, Jesus is our gate to salvation. If we do not go through Him we are lost.

Every day in our life we meet signs of death. Many of our teenage friends are getting involved in drugs, gangs, violence, and terrorism. Because they choose the wrong gate, they are lost. Watching these tragic events, we can easily lose hope that our lives will not be fulfilling. Sometimes we would like to escape the real world. We wish we could go to Paradise where there is no fear, no anger, no sadness, and no hatred. All these thoughts are nothing but signs of death in today's world.

Our friend, Jesus told us *"I have come that they may have life and have it to the fullest"* (John10: 10). Jesus Christ brought us a new and abundant life that we have to reveal to the hopeless world. As teenagers, you have a great desire to live, to learn, and to do many things. You want to discover the secrets of life. You want to travel around the world and meet new people. These are your hopes and desires for a new and rich life. You have to live these desires for the common benefits of your community; to make peace and justice in the world; and you have to share these desires and hopes with others. These are signs of the abundant and new life which our friend Jesus invites us to implement in this world.

We will suffer and experience seasons of hopelessness in our life, because life is an adventure. There is death, there is sickness, and there is sorrow. However, these challenges cannot destroy the values of fraternity, friendship, and solidarity that inspire us to meet, help each other, and build the new and abundant life that our friend Jesus brought to us. In this confused world, Jesus declares, "You can take heart because I have overcome the world. If you put your trust and hope in Me, then we will overcome all this pain, and we will overcome death."

In 1992, during the Summer Olympics in Barcelona, Spain, the favorite to win the gold medal in the 400-meter run was a young man named Derek Redmond. Derek was 26-years old. In the middle of his race Derek fell flat on the track. When he fought his way back to his feet he grabbed the back of his leg in pain. A torn hamstring had brought a lifetime of dreams to a miserable end in a split second. But Derek got up. He began hopping around that track on one leg. When he reached the home stretch a large man broke through the security guards and onto the track. The man put his arms around Derek and together they hobbled toward the finish line. It turned out that the man was Derek's father, Jim Redmond. It made a beautiful picture. There was a fallen hero and a loving father making sure that he finished the race strongly. Everyone who watched on television that day will never forget that scene.

Derek Redmond is a picture of some of us. Some of us are lying on the track of life with our dreams smashed and our hopes dashed. Setbacks are not easy. But look, from out of the stands comes a loving Father who takes our arm and puts it over His own shoulder. He will see us to the finish line if we will walk with Him! Like Derek we have a hope. Do not give up, be persistent.

Application

- What are the signs of the new and abundant life?
- Do you remember a story in which you announced the new life in this confused world?
- What are the signs of death in your church, school, and country? What are your suggestions to overcome these signs?

Supplication of Saint Jacob

The Son,
Who by His Cross delivered the Church from error,
grant her Your peace,
and keep her children by the Cross of light.

May the peace,
which reconciled those in heaven with those on earth,
bring peace to Your Church,
and keep her children by the Cross of light.

Son of God,
in whose Cross the creation rejoiced,
let my mind rejoice in the Cross of light,
on which You were hung.
As You have made me worthy, Lord,
to speak of the Cross of the light,
make me worthy of the wedding banquets of Your Church,
which was saved by it.
Great Savior,
Who saved Your Church from error,
save me in my weakness
on the day when the just judgment is given.
On this festival we are assembled before Your Cross;
on the eternal festival,
may I see Your compassion and praise your name. Amen.

This supplication is said during the third hour of Friday in the common prayer

Fourth Station

THE HOLY CHURCH

"When He was at the table with them, He took bread, gave thanks, broke it and began to give it to them. Then their eyes were open, and they recognized Him"

(Luke 24: 30 – 31).

We have arrived at the last station of our journey: *the Holy Church*.

As we read in the story of the disciples of Emmaus, Jesus Christ talked to the disciples all the way from Jerusalem to Emmaus, preparing them to enter the house. When they entered and sat at the table, He blessed and broke the bread. They then immediately recognized Him.

This station will conduct you to enter the house of God, which is the Church, sit at the table, and learn who founded the Church. What are the elements that form the Church? What is the mission of the Church? And what are the fundamental signs of the Church?

1. The Foundation of the Church

When we studied the second part of this journey, we saw that the people of the Old Testament were waiting for a new hope, and a new alliance. In the story of "the liberation from Egypt," we learned that Christ is a new Moses and the Church is the new people of the alliance, born from the death, burial and resurrection of our Lord Jesus Christ.

The Church was founded by Jesus Christ. It is, and it will be, animated by the Holy Spirit. The first Christian Church of the apostles understood this idea. Jesus Christ promised to send His Holy Spirit to animate the Church He founded. We read in the *Acts of the Apostles* that Jesus asked them, "Not to leave Jerusalem but wait for the gift My Father promised." After they would receive the power of the Holy Spirit, they would be His witnesses in Jerusalem and in all Judea and Samaria, and to the ends of the earth (turn to, Acts 1: 4 – 8).

The first disciples stayed in Jerusalem waiting for the promises and, "When the day of Pentecost came, they were all together in one place. Suddenly a sound like the blowing of violent wind came from heaven and filled the whole house where they were sitting. They saw what seemed to be tongues of fire that separated and came to rest on each of them. All of them were filled with the Holy Spirit and began to speak in other tongues as the Spirit enabled them" (Acts 2: 1 – 4).

The Church has recognized this event as an extraordinary manifestation of the people of the new covenant which is characterized by the unceasing presence of the Holy Spirit.

On that day, the Church of the apostles would recognize

its own mission, which is, *to proclaim that all people are called to build a family through the Risen Jesus Christ.*

The event of the descent of the Holy Spirit on the first disciples reveals that *the Church was founded, not according to human expectations, but it was founded by God, born by His initiative and promoted by His Holy Spirit.*

The Foundation of the Church

The Church was founded, not according to a human expectations, but by God, born by His initiative and promoted by His Holy Spirit.

The Mission of the Church

To proclaim that all people are called to build a universal family through the Risen Jesus Christ

When an individual becomes a member of the Church, a new relationship is born. That person is enfolded spiritually into the family of God. The bond is described by Jesus as that of being like a bride coming into relationship with her husband. An understanding of love and shared intimacy is gained that had been unknown before the bonding of that relationship, one to the other. Therefore, the Church of Christ is not an organization, but rather a description of the living relationship between the Risen Christ and those who have turned their hearts over to Him.

Supplication

You are blessed, O Church,
to whom the word of the Son is a protection,
and the bars of hell shall not prevail against you henceforth and forever.

He gave you His Flesh to eat and His Blood,
The Chalice of Salvation is pardon for your Children.

Earth, earth hear the Word of the Lord God,
who swore to His Church,
I will not forsake you forever.

Your walls, O faithful Church, are before me at all times,
and I myself will dwell within you.

Virgin Mother of God, repair our broken hearts,
for on every side the waves and storms beat upon us.

You have confidence before God,
beg of Him, by your prayers, to show mercy to us;
to give health to those who are sick,
and refreshment to those who are weary,
and return to those who are far away,
and to us forgiveness of offences. Amen.

2. The Church is One Body Animated by the Holy Spirit

The Book of Acts, in its first chapters, teaches us how the first Christian Church lived. The disciples "devoted themselves to the apostles' teaching and fellowship, to the breaking of bread and to prayer. Everyone was filled with awe, and many wonders and miraculous signs were done by the apostles. All the believers were together and had everything in common. Selling their possessions and goods, they gave to anyone as he had need. Every day they continued to meet together in the Temple courts. They broke bread in their homes and ate together with glad and sincere hearts, praising God and enjoying the favor of all the people. And the Lord added to their number daily those who were being saved" (Acts 2: 42 – 48).

Nurtured by the Word of God, the community of the disciples lived in a fraternity and unity. The first day after the Sabbath, the disciples used to celebrate the Holy Eucharist together, and together they prayed in their homes.

In reading this passage from the Book of the Acts, we learn that *the loyalty to the Word of God (scriptures), the fraternal communion, the Holy Eucharist, and prayer are the signs of unity in any Christian community.*

In this community we find diversity of services and gifts. Each one of us should work to build the Church. St. Paul, in his letter to the Ephesians, says: "It was He who gave some to be apostles, some to be prophets, some to be evangelists, and some to be pastors and teachers, to prepare God's people for works of service, so that the body of Christ may be built up until we all reach unity" (Ephesians, 4: 11–12).

The Signs of Unity

The loyalty to the Word of God (scriptures), the fraternal communion, the Holy Eucharist, and prayer are the signs of unity in any Christian community.

The Church embodies individuals in relationship with Christ, seeking to be the very presence of Christ in the lives of others and within society. It is the coming together of these individuals which forms the Church as St. Paul describes it in his first letter to the Corinthians, *"the body of Christ."* Paul is noting that as individual members of the body we each bring our gifts and abilities to contribute to the body as a whole, "if the ear should say, because I'm not an eye, I do not belong to the body, it would not for that reason cease to be a part of the body" (I Corinthians 12: 16). In the same way, each member of the Church, which is the body of Christ, brings his or her contribution; no one more or less important than any other. We actualize this unity when the word of God is proclaimed and the Lord's Supper is distributed and given to each one of us.

The one body animated by the Holy Spirit is revealed also in the parish, where we meet every Sunday all together, children, youth and adults, around the Word of God and the Lord's Supper. Together we praise and give thanks to God, we meet as a family of God, we share our concerns and ambitions, and we are united in the Body of Christ. St. Paul explains this idea in his first letter to the Corinthians saying: "Is not the cup of thanksgiving for which we give thanks a *participation* in the blood of Christ? And is not the bread that we break a *participation* in the body of Christ? Because there is one loaf, we, who are many, are one body, for we all partake of the one loaf" (1Corinthian 10:16).

The division of the church

Today, Christians are divided: Catholic, Orthodox, Protestants, Anglicans...etc. Although they all refer to the Gospel, they belong to different traditions and confessions.

Jesus Christ prayed for the unity of His own disciples, "That all of them may be one, Father just as You are in Me and I am in You" (John 17: 21). Why have divisions entered the Church? The answer is difficult. We have to think over the journey of the Church to understand the various historical and political reasons that created the various divisions in the Christian community. However, the main issue that caused the division is *sin*, which is always present. Often the divisions and conflicts are revealed when Christian faith is not under persecution, and when human interest suffocates God's gifts.

With the beginning of this century, under the guidance of the Holy Spirit, various Christian churches started the *Ecumenical Movement. Ecumenism,* or *Ecumenical,* is an adjective derived from the Greek language; it means the idea that promotes uniting different parts of the Christian faith. This movement has promoted many ideas, meetings, and conventions to eliminate the gaps between Christian churches.

How can we contribute to the Ecumenical Movement?

There is no real ecumenism if it is not accompanied by *conversion and humility.* The desire for unity starts by renewing our hearts, and by submitting ourselves, in humility, to the Spirit of the Lord who wanted all His followers to be one. Thus, Ecumenism is the fruit of committed prayers and exchanged love. To live in Ecumenical spirit we are called to live in dialogue with all. This dialogue should be in harmony with the values of the Gospel, which guide us to a desired unity.

Ecumenism, however, does not mean eliminating our traditions and religious values and denying our particular religious identity. Ecumenism means living in love and having respect for others. It means learning about our faith and the faith of others, focusing on the elements that unite us, not the aspects that separate us. The Spirit of Ecumenism is the spirit of prayer, love and acceptance. It means accepting others, as people created in God's Image, and recognizing them as brothers and sisters in Christ. It is also the spirit of discernment. We have to discern which are the churches and denominations that are guided by the Spirit of the Lord. St. Paul in his first letter to Corinthians instructs us to detect, by the Spirit of the Lord, all the teachings that we are exposed to, "The man without the spirit does not accept things that come from the Spirit of God, for they are foolishness to him, and he cannot understand them, because they are spiritually discerned. The spiritual man makes judgments about all things, but he himself is not subject to any man's judgment: 'for who has known the mind of the Lord that he may instruct him?' But we have the mind of Christ" (I Corinthians 2:14-15).

Jesus prayed for the unity of His believers

I pray for those who will believe in Me...
That all of them may be one,

Father just as You are in Me and I am in You.
May they also be in Us
so that the world may believe that You have sent Me.

I have given them the glory that You gave Me,
that they may be one as We are One:
I in them and You in Me.

May they be brought to complete unity,
to let the world know that You sent Me,
and have loved them even as You have loved Me.

Father, I want those You have given Me to be with Me where I am,
and to see My glory You have given Me,
because You loved Me before the creation of the world.

> Righteous Father,
> though the world does not know You, I know You,
> and they know that You have sent Me.
>
> I have made You known to them,
> and will continue to make You known,
> in order that the love You have for Me may be in them,
> and that I Myself may be in them.
>
> (John 17: 21 – 26).

Discuss with your Friends

- We have read a few passages from the book of the Acts of the Apostles. We learned the fundamental elements that form any Christian community. Discuss in your group:
  - What was the lifestyle of the first Christian church?
  - How can you relate them to your parish?
  - How can you promote these aspects in your church?
  - Try to think of a project that will promote, in your church, the fraternal communion, prayer, loyalty to the Word of God, and participation in the Holy Eucharist.
- How can we promote and live in Christian unity?

> By Your Cross, Lord, the Church was redeemed
> and, in it, she boasts,
> and by the sufferings of the Cross she is raised on high.
> Keep us, Lord, who have taken refuge in the Cross,
> from the evil one and his power, halleluiah,
>
> Keep us Lord, beneath the wings of Your Cross.
>
> *This prayer is said on Friday morning*

What did you learn from this station?

We can summarize what we learned in this last station in two important points.

1. The church is a visible people and invisible fellowship

What came into existence as a result of the acts of Jesus, briefly examined, was a visible community of the people of the New Testament. This community is united by visible bonds which are: 1) The Word of God, preached by the apostles, and accepted and publicly professed in faith; 2) participation in the Lord's Supper, for which baptism is the initiation and the distinctive community act of worship of the new church; 3) fellowship with the apostles.

This new common life in the Body of Christ is the substance of the messianic blessings that the people of the Old Testament so eagerly awaited. In it is fulfilled the celebrated prophecy of Jeremiah, "This is the covenant I will make with the house of Israel after that time, declares the Lord. I will put My law in their minds and write it on their hearts. I will be their God and they will be My people" (Jeremiah 31: 33).

The outward fellowship of the Church is of value only in so far as it expresses and promotes this inner communion with Christ. These functions are an indispensable, integral, inseparable part of the Church Christ formed.

2. Common life in the Spirit

The Church possesses its own characteristic way of life which is defined with reference to the Holy Spirit Who animates it. The way of life of God's people is life in the Spirit. This is the direct opposite of the selfish, sinful life which is ours by nature, as St. Paul terms it, "according to the flesh." It is the work of the Spirit to overcome this fleshy life by implanting in men's hearts the love of Christ. The Spirit creates the "new spiritual man" whose life is the outgoing, self-sacrificing life of redemptive love communicated to him by the risen Christ. As Christ delivered Himself from death "for the redemption of many," so the Christian is, by definition, one who accepts responsibility for the salvation of others and does not refuse to carry their burdens. The Christian life consists of an unending series of "spiritual sacrifices" which are prayer, almsgiving, penance, witness, and good works of all kinds. These are the sacrifices the Christian offers as the normal fruits of life in the Church.

It is much desired that we recover the vivid experience of possessing the Spirit enjoyed by the early Christians, that we become more deeply aware of life in Christ as life in Christ's Spirit. In this way, our Christian existence will become the vital and dynamic reality it ought to be, the source of joy, peace, gentleness, kindness, confidence and all the other "fruits of the Spirit," which characterize the Christian.

I would like to conclude with the exhortation of St. Paul to Colossians,

> "Therefore, as God's chosen people,
>
> holy and dearly loved,
>
> clothe yourselves, with compassion, kindness, humility, gentleness and patience.
>
> Bear with each other and forgive whatever grievances you may have against one another.
>
> Forgive as the Lord forgave you.
>
> And, over all these virtues, put on love, which binds them all together in perfect unity.
>
> Let the peace of Christ rule in your hearts,

since, as members of one body, you were called to peace.

And be thankful.

Let the Word of Christ dwell in you richly

as you teach and admonish one another with all wisdom,

and as you sing psalms, hymns and spiritual songs

with gratitude in your hearts to God.

And whatever you do, whether in word or deed,

do it all in the name of the Lord Jesus,

giving thanks to God the Father through Him.

(Colossians 3: 12 – 17).

Conclusion

We have arrived at the conclusion of the Emmaus journey. We passed through four stations, encountered many figures from the Bible, prayed together, and were instructed about the real sense and meaning of Scripture.

We did not want to learn only information about the Bible, or about the teachings and the theology of the Church. That was a distant goal of this journey. The main purpose is to have a transformed heart and to learn how to build an intimate relationship with our Lord Jesus Christ.

You might have heard about the Bible and Jesus. You might have read a few passages from the Bible and learned some of its stories. But that is not enough. You need to experience and live out your Christian life, you need to witness to the world about your faith, you need to live by conviction, not by merely belief alone.

In the beginning of their journey, we read how Jesus scolded the two disciples for not believing, "How *foolish* you are, and how *slow of heart* to believe" (Luke 24: 25). But later on, as the story continues, and as their walk with Jesus became more intimate, we saw a changing in their hearts, "Were not our *hearts burning* within us while He talked and opened the scriptures to us" (Luke 24: 32). They experience a heart transformation from a "slow heart" to a "burning one."

Did you experience this transformation during this journey. Did you shout as the two disciples did, "was not my heart burning within me while I was reading and discussing this journey." If not, then you need to open your heart to Christ and ask Him to renew the power, the gifts, and the anointing of the Holy Spirit that lives within you .

Going to church and socializing is not enough, practicing sacraments is not enough. You need an Emmaus journey.

Our Christian faith is not about behavior modification or some practices, it is about heart transformation.

During this journey we learned that the Word of God is a "seed," which when fallen into good soil, produces fruitful and multiple crops. The soil is our heart; if the soil is not prepared to receive the Word of God, the seed will be suffocated and die.

In the parable of the sower, Jesus tells us that there are four kinds of soils, or hearts: 1) *The hard path*, "Those along the path are the ones who hear, and then the devil comes and takes away the Word from their hearts, so they may not believe and be saved" (Luke 8: 12). 2) *The rocky path*, "Those on the rock are the ones who receive the word with joy when they hear it, but they have no root. They believe for a while, but in the time of testing they fall away" (Luke 8: 13). 3) *The thorny path*, "The seed that fell among the thorns stands for those who hear but as they go on their way they are choked by life's worries, riches and pleasures, and they do not mature" (Luke 8: 14). 4) *The good soil*, "But the seed on good soil stands for those with noble and good hearts, who hear the word, retain it, and by preserving produce a crop" (Luke 8: 15).

Which one is your heart? Where did the seed of this journey fall? Did you notice some changing crops in your heart? If not, ask the Lord to come into your heart and cleanse it in order to become good soil; ask the Lord to take out all the thorns, the rocks, the pleasure, the worries, that hinder the seed to grow and produce good fruit. It is never too late. Don't be discouraged. Remember, we learned that Jesus is your friend, Who loves you, cares about you and brings you new and plentiful life.

Let's give thanks to the Lord for this journey.

In the name of the Father, the Son, and the Holy Spirit, One true God, to Whom be glory and upon us mercy and compassion for ever and ever. Amen

We give You thanks o Lord,
because You have become a part of our human story
and where You established in us a New Alliance.
With Abraham, Jacob, Joseph, and all the Prophets,
You taught us to hope for salvation.

We give You thanks o Lord
because You, so much loved the world
to send Your only-Begotten Son, Jesus the Savior.
He is God,
Who is our friend,
Who guides us in life,
and through the Holy Spirit He creates in us a new heart.

We thank You o Lord,
for the death and resurrection of Jesus Christ,
because through it we become a New Creature.

We thank You O Lord
because in Your church we are a family,
gathered by the power of the Holy Spirit,
to recognize and love the image of Christ
in every man and woman.

We thank You o Lord
because Your Holy Spirit created in us new eyes,
that can see the needs and sufferance of our brothers and sisters.
We thank you o Lord
because, through the gift of the New birth, you created in us a new spirit
that can infuse the light in the darkness

We thank You o Lord
because we are Your sons and daughters
created in Your image,
and we are moved by the gifts of Your Holy Spirit,
which is the Spirit of Faith, Love, and Hope. Amen.

Fr. Abjar Bahkou